FUNNY HO HO AND FUNNY FANTASTIC

By the same author

FUNNY HA HA AND FUNNY PECULIAR
FUNNY CONVULSING AND FUNNY CONFUSING

FUNNY HO HO AND FUNNY FANTASTIC

DENYS PARSONS

A PAN ORIGINAL

PAN BOOKS LTD : LONDON

First published 1967 by
PAN BOOKS LTD.,
33 Tothill Street, London, S W 1

ISBN 0 330 10670 8

2nd Printing 1968
3rd Printing 1973

Printed in Great Britain by
Cox and Wyman Limited, London
Reading and Fakenham

INTRODUCTION

The success of *Funny Ha Ha and Funny Peculiar* was most encouraging, and I am grateful to readers who have sent in contributions for this eighth collection of items inspired by that supreme creative humorist, Gobfrey Shrdlu.

For those unfamiliar with the way in which newspapers are put together, I must explain that the compositor's keyboard is not the familiar QWERTYUIOP, but is laid out in groups of six, beginning S H R D L U – the origin of our hero's name. Nobody has disputed my claim that Gobfrey Shrdlu is the evil genius who causes all the misprints and howlers which plague printers and sub-editors. Shrdlu also undoubtedly has a hand in bringing about certain strange happenings, oddities, freak accidents, and absurdities which are reported in the Press.

As before, I have arranged, for your enjoyment, howlers and misprints (Funny Ho Ho) on the left-hand pages, oddities and absurdities (Funny Fantastic) on the right-hand pages.

My thanks are due to the editors of *Punch*, the *New Yorker*, and *Everywoman*, and to Macdonald & Co (Publishers) Ltd, for permission to use material, and to many others who have waived copyright. My thanks too to an indefatigable shrdlologist, Mr Edward North of Sidcup.

Funny Ho Ho

Funny Fantastic

Before Miss Jenkinson concluded the concert by singing 'I'll walk beside you' she was prevented with a bouquet of red roses.

Sussex paper

FATHER OF TEN SHOT DEAD

. . .

Mistaken for rabbit

Headline in New York paper

A familiar question was re-opened – How Sunday School children are to be attached to the Church, and once more the use of adhesive stamps was recommended.

New Zealand Church News

A big music store in the centre of Louisville has been completely burned out. The fire-brigade played on the burning instruments for many hours.

Northern Daily Mail

'Who shall say howqztNj wodrmf?'

Manchester Daily Despatch

Students who marry during their course will not be permitted to remain in college. Further, students who are already married must either live with their husbands or make other arrangements with the dean.

Syllabus of an Ohio College

PROFITABLE but eerie business is being worked up by 12-year-old Wayne Marmorstein of Nutley, New Jersey . . . eight-legged frogs.

Since he first found his strange frogs in a mudhole near his home and sold them to a scientist for 21s., researchers are bidding for all he can catch. 'From now on they'll have to pay more,' says little businessman Wayne.

Daily Express

A 30-year-old housewife – accused of stealing two tins of meat from a supermarket – told Leamington magistrates that she had 'never been the same' since she saw a man running about in the nude. 'I have been under sedatives from my doctor ever since,' she said.

Leamington Morning News quoted in *New Statesman*

Tight-rope walkers Roger and Betty Decugis, who wanted their five-month-old daughter Christine christened on a high wire slung 400 ft over Somerset's Cheddar Gorge, have had their idea turned down by the Bishop of Clifton, the Rt Rev. Joseph Rudderham. Now their daughter will be christened in church – and then will be taken across the wire on a motor-cycle.

Daily Express

The marriage has taken place quietly in England between the Earl of Selborne and Mrs Valerie de Thomka de tomkahaza et folkusfalva, daughter of the late J. A. de Thomka de tomkahaza et folkusfalva and Baronesse Irene de Thomka de tomkahaza et folkusfalva.

Daily Telegraph

HAVE A BABY?
Read **HOW TO GET FATHER TO HELP**

On cover of *My baby magazine*

CORRECTION – *In page four of story catchlined 'Libraries' line five please read 'were like crustacea', etc., thus substituting 'crustacea' for 'Crewe Station'.*

News Agency tape

Had it not been for the so-called 'die-hards' – a term so often referred to us Nationalists disparagingly, yet so invigorating to all those who do not betray principles – who have unfailingly sustained the European theory of our now muddled thinking on 'European theory' of our ethnological existence, by now muddled thinking on this subject would have been more general and deep-rooted.

Times of Malta

Mr and Mrs Simon Parker request the honour of your presents at the marriage of their daughter Eve to Mr James Turner.

Wedding invitation

Alderman M. Bloom: There you have a classic example of how by question and answer an innuendo is freely displayed in the Council Chamber, blown sky-high, and brought back as a boomerang on the people who tried to set it alight.

Yorks paper

4 SINGLE POUND NOTES LOST, 27th Jan., vicinity Market St; sentimental value; reward.

Advert in Aberdeen paper

Every time 33-year-old Mrs Alice Longson had a bath the telephone rang in the hall. Each time she ran downstairs to answer it. Each time there was no caller on the line. Mrs Longson at first thought it was the work of a practical joker. But it happened again and again. Always at bathtime.

She called in telephone engineers. They could not find a fault. So Mrs Longson's husband, Leo, 53, tried to find the answer himself. He ripped out wires and fuses in their converted cottage at Maxey, near Stamford, Lincolnshire. At last he found the trouble; the immersion heater which heated only the bath water had rotted and some of the electric current was leaking away to earth. And that caused the phone to ring downstairs.

Mrs Longson said: 'I ought to have guessed. We had similar trouble a year ago with a faulty plate on my electric cooker. But then the phone rang every time I cooked the dinner.'

Daily Mail

A woman mourner was horrified when her best hat was buried with the coffin at a South African funeral – she had planned to wear it to a cocktail party later in the day, but an undertaker mistook it for a floral tribute.

Weekend

The night David Dann murdered his wife their lodger, Bertram Johnston, heard a shot. But he did not leave his bedroom to find out what was the matter. 'I assumed Mrs Dann was being assaulted,' he explained yesterday, 'and I had no wish to get involved.'

Daily Express

Will the parents of the boy who gave a little boy an apple in exchange for his tricycle outside the Sale Lido on Friday between 6 and 7, kindly return it at once?

Advert in *Manchester Evening News*

The Mayor then raised the punch bowl to his lips, remarking: 'And now prosperity to all the people of B—, and prospezity to uor godo old tiwn. (Applause).

Report of local function

Soloist At the Trinity Y.P.U. meeting referred to on Saturday, Miss McCausland sang the solo, Lord Speak To Me, not Miss McDonald.

Canadian paper

In 1918 Miss G— joined the New Zealand Army Nursing Service as a masseuse. She has served on several local bodies.

New Zealand paper

We wish to state clearly that we have no need to plagiarize, our staff being sufficiently competent to stand upon its own bottom.

Trade paper

Miss Polly R—, the home centre forward, was continually bursting down the middle.

Yorkshire Post

Mr and Mrs John Nash Wilding, of 880 Fifth Avenue, announce the engagement of their debatable daughter, Miss Virgin A. Wilding, to Mr Luis Marcellino de Acevedo of Buenos Aires.

New York Tribune

Mrs Thurston Longson and daughters are planning to tour the Black Hills, Yellowstone Park and other places of interest. They are taking a tent and cooking utensils and will vamp by the side of the road.

South Dakota paper

90 YEARS MAIL IN ONE DELIVERY

BELGRADE, December 9. – *The new owner of a house at Pancevo, near here, opened the lower shutters in front of a walled-in window – and unopened letters, telegrams, and newspapers dating back 90 years fell out. All that time postmen had been dropping mail through an open upper shutter thinking there was a glass pane behind it.*

Mrs Vera Aremovic said her grandfather and father, both merchants with extensive connections throughout the Austro-Hungarian Empire, lived in the house. Their businesses failed because trading partners complained that they never answered letters.

Reuter

ONE MEETS SUCH CURIOUS PEOPLE
WHEN ONE HOPS ON A PLANE TO MOROCCO

Headline in Sunday paper

The most bizarre insurance claim of the year is due to be lodged by a London motorist. The claim will be for damage to a stationary car. It was hit by a lavatory.

The unlikely incident occurred yesterday morning outside the National Film Theatre on London's South Bank. The motorist found the wing of his car had been struck by a mobile convenience which was being towed into position for display. The mobile lavatories are manufactured by a laundry firm for use at race meetings and other outdoor events.

Daily Mirror

A man, alleged to have been caught stealing six chickens from a butcher's shop, was said to have told the police: 'I was taking them home to throw at the wife. We've had a row.'

News of the World

Mr Jenkins, it is claimed, was driving at a high rate of speed and swerving from side to side. As he approached the crossing he started directly towards it and crashed into Miss Miller's rear end which was sticking out into the road about a foot. Luckily she escaped injury and the damage can be easily remedied with a new coat of paint.

Pomeroy (*Ohio*) *Democrat*

MODEL WILLING TO
POSE FOR NUDE ARTIST

Card in shop window

Dear Mum,

just a card to say I arrived alrite and if you don't know my address write and arsk me for it and I will send it to you.

Love, Alfie

Letter from cadet in camp

With the advent of spring, the carpet beetle commences its ravenous inroads into your carpets. Have them treated now before irreparable damage is done by the Nelson firm with 10 years guarantee.

Advert in *Nelson Evening Mail*

Plump, crew-cut, blinking a little behind black-rimmed spectacles, Allan Sherman was born in Chicago in 1924.

Radio Times

MARACAIBO. Venezuela, Monday. Ines Maria Cuervo, 35-year-old mother of five, has been told by doctors here that she will give birth to quintuplets shortly.

The quins' father is a 39-year-old father of eight. Both are so pleased that before the quins arrive they plan to marry.

Daily Mail

WANTED: Fifty Chinese Abacus Operators.

An English businessman is offering £15-a-week jobs to 50 Chinese who can operate an abacus, a counting device invented by the Chinese more than 10,000 years ago. He is Mr Gerald Leanse, 55-year-old managing director of Faxi-Foto Typesetting Equipment, of Seymour-place, Marylebone, London.

His typesetter is unable to make each line of type end in the same place. Mr Leanse believes that this job, known in the trade as justifying, could be done more cheaply and much more quickly than by a £500,000 computer. He said: 'The operators would be fed information in the same way as a computer. Each letter of the alphabet or character would be represented by so many beads on the abacus. In this way we could find within seconds where to end each line of type.'

Mr Leanse began his attempt to find abacus experts by advertising in *The Times*. So far no one has come forward. He said: 'I doubt very much whether there are any in this country. But I am quite willing to import them from China or Hongkong, and pay their fares.'

Daily Mail

Proudly drum-major Steve Harding threw his baton twirling into the air. And all at once a 10-block area in Ventura, California town, was blacked out, a radio station went dead, and a grass fire started. The baton had hit two 4,000 volt power lines. The baton melted.

Daily Express

Applications are invited for superintendent for the making of nurses' uniforms. Successful candidate must have knowledge of upholstery.

Advert in *Daily Mail*

An opportunity occurs in a large and rapidly expanding firm of floor tile manufacturers and contractors for a representative to cover the Yorkshire and North Eastern Districts.

Advert in *The Guardian*

A carpet was stolen last night from Ryde Council building. Measuring almost 6 feet square, the thief has baffled council officers.

Sydney, Australia, paper

A study by three physicians showed that perhaps two out of three births in the U.S result from pregnancies.

Columbus (*Ohio*) *Citizen*

A few years ago all a charmer had to do was offer his snake basket and camera-carrying tourists would fall in from every direction.

Weekend

Ghana is to change over to driving on the right. The change will be made gradually.

Ghana Paper

INSTRUCTIONS

Pour a teaspoonful of the
shampoo into the palm
of each hand . . .

Label on bottle

Miss Smith told the *Evening Standard* today: 'He hit me on the temple with his fist, and I was knocked into the ditch. While I was lying there dazed something made me say to him: "Thanks very much!" He replied in quite a refined accent: "Oh, don't mention it."'

Evening Standard

PARIS, October 2 – *An unknown woman who fell from a tower of Notre Dame cathedral today landed on an American, Veronica McConnell, aged 22, of Philadelphia. Both were killed. Miss McConnell arrived here last night in a tour party of 40.*

Reuter

A letter addressed to 'Degenerate Bawd' in London has been correctly deciphered by the Post Office as being intended for the Central Electricity Generating Board, according to the February issue of *Power News.*

Evening Standard

MANURE HEAP POSES BORDER PROBLEM

Hermannsreuth, October 29. – Czechoslovak officials have been asked to make a slight alteration in the border with West Germany – so that farmer Josef Dill can get to his manure heap. The border runs across farmer Dill's land, and for years the Czechoslovaks have turned a blind eye when he and his wife crossed the border to get to the heap and to use their outside toilet.

But recently they ordered him to move the manure and said that in future they would only permit border crossings to the toilet. Because farmer Dill has nowhere else to put the manure, German Customs officials are asking the Czechoslovaks to allow the border to make a small detour round the heap.

The Guardian

This summer the Graham family – father, mother and teenage daughter – will move into the bungalow which they have planned and built themselves from books borrowed from their local library.

Sunday Express

There is also a very good instant, non-fat skimmed milk powder on the market, made by Blank's. A 3s. 3d. packet is equal to eight pints; it is tasteless in coffee or tea, very good for moulds and blancmange.

The Lady

However, do persevere with the bleaching treatment for it may do the trick: simply apply lemon juice to the skin, every night and mourning for a fortnight.

She

Send mother a gift of hardly ever blooming rose bushes.

Sioux Falls Argus Leader

The Crewe committee has arranged to apply the vaccine to 20 calves in October and three months later five or six more will be inoculated. Later, some of both lots will be killed for the post-mortem examination, and if it is likely to prove beneficial, human beings will be similarly treated.

Australian paper

Judge Hall said: 'I consider that this case is in the shadows – if I had not received a "not guilty" plea, I would not have been surprised. And I think it would have been upheld.'

He added: 'I start work next week on a new film, called *Diabolique*. I will play a patriotic gangster.'

Daily Mirror

I have bad news today for artists who want to use the distinctive Asphaltum brown favoured by the pre-Raphaelites. C. Roberson, the Camden Town colour maker, has run out of mummies.

'We may have a few odd limbs lying around somewhere, but not enough to make any more Asphaltum,' said Mr Geoffrey Roberson-Park, the managing director. 'We sold our last complete mummy some years ago for, I think, £3. Perhaps we shouldn't have done. We certainly can't get any more.'

These were, after all, no ordinary mummies, but the remains of Indian priests of a minor order preserved in a rare type of bitumen. Chipped off and powdered, it made a paint superior to others containing bitumen: it did not distort the canvas by contracting. Roberson-Park, who has been with the family firm only 43 of its 160 years, is not sure when the mummies were bought. It was probably in the 1870s, when brown was popular. Roberson's Asphaltum can still be easily distinguished from other people's in the works of such artists as Burne-Jones, Holman Hunt and Millais. It is the Asphaltum that hasn't cracked.

Financial Times

DON'T THROW
PEOPLE BELOW

Notice on Southend pier

A second-hand car dealer in Connecticut has learned that it doesn't pay to use slang in advertising. He advertised a 1962 Pontiac for '1,395 bananas' (slang for dollars). When a housewife offered him 25 bananas on deposit, he refused to accept it. The housewife sued, alleged false advertising, and won her case. She presented the dealer with the balance of bananas and drove the car away.

Sunday Times

He was opposed to a fence round Japan and letting her stew in her own juice, as it would create a festering sore with permanent explosive tendencies.

A speaker quoted in *The Times*

CONCEIVED in the summer of 1959, the 38-year-old Managing Director J. G. Robinson (known in the motoring world as Jeff) has watched this model develop after being throughly tested in the Welsh mountains.

Advert in *The Queen*

TWO YEARS BEFORE THE MAST
Alan Ladd, Brian Donlevy.

The action-filled story of a shanghaied crew on a trip around the Matterhorn in the 1880s.

Fort Lauderdale News

I would like to warn readers to obtain some references before employing hitherto unknown people to do work for them. I have been bitten by one – HOUSEHOLDER.

Liverpool Echo

The Chinese believe that the object of the Japanese warships is to cover possible landing of troops with a view to the Sandwichiang of the Chinese forces attacking Wuhu.

Scottish paper

A JUGGLER GLUED ME TO MY DECK CHAIR

Headline in *The Sun*

Sports car, preferably foreign, wanted weekend 22 June by respectable middle-aged civil servant, to raise son's status at preparatory school where most fathers have Jaguars.

Advert in *The Times*

A neurotic man who, during periodic fits of depression, takes his false teeth out and jumps on them, is to get half the cost of a new set from Dorset Health Committee 'on the grounds of hardship'.

News Chronicle quoted in *New Statesman*

Middlesex County Council is to be represented in Twickenham Fair procession by West Middlesex main drainage department. It is exhibiting a tableau of three decorated vehicles depicting the stages through which sewage passes.

Surrey Comet quoted in *New Statesman*

'*Dear Milkman: Starting today leave one Jersey on Mondays and Thursdays but none on Saturday – then leave 1 thick cream on Tuesdays and 1 yoghourt on Wednesdays with 1 quart of Jersey. Then leave 1 quart of Jersey on Friday with thick cream, for the weekends leave 2 Jerseys and 1 yoghourt on a Saturday and 1 thick cream on a Sunday. Please alternate this for me. If the thick cream falls on a Saturday leave 1 Jersey with it then. Empty bottles are in the garage. Climb through the side window. Garage is locked.*'

Shirley Glick in *Reader's Digest*

Le Capitaine Soames, en uniforme des Cold Cream Guards, attendait sa fiancée.

French paper

Dear Madam,

With reference to your blue raincoat, our manufacturers have given the garment in question a thorough testing, and find that it is absolutely waterproof. If you will wear it on a dry day, and then take it off and examine it you will see that our statement is correct.

Your obedient servants,
Bank & Co, Drapers

100 NEW PRICE RISES

But grocers say they will not
hit the housewives

The Sun

News From The Hospitals
Admitted: Gay Tufarolo, 107 Main Street.
Discouraged: Mrs Elizabeth Cook, Holly Hill.

Daytona Beach Evening News

We require a first-class man for rubbing-up and making good concrete faces.

Advert in *Leicester Mercury*

Elizabeth found herself on a stool by the nursery fire. Securely pierced by a long brass toasting-fork she held a square piece of bread to the glowing flameless fire.

Women's magazine

GEORGE CRAWLS UNDER A HIPPO ON THE A33

It was all part of the job, but it put George Hawarth flat on his back yesterday under a hippopotamus called Douglas. Mr Hawarth, 56-year-old Ministry of Transport examiner, reappeared unscathed after three minutes. 'A rather unusual experience,' he commented dryly.

The man from the Ministry and the hippo came almost face to face on the A33 during a check on lorries leaving Southampton. Police signalled a five-ton lorry driven by John Goddard into a layby. Mr Hawarth, 14 years a vehicle inspector, who lives in Hayes, Middlesex, slipped underneath the lorry with Douglas only a few inches above him.

The Zoo owner James Chipperfield arrived and said: 'Excuse me, but you are lying under a hippopotamus, which weighs nearly a ton and gets upset if he is not frequently hosed with water to keep cool.' Said Mr Hawarth: 'Fortunately the lorry was in fairly good condition and the check took a short time.' Mr Chipperfield explained: 'Douglas would have become restive if he got overheated. The wind as the lorry drives along helps cool him and during the trip to York he was sprayed four times with water.'

Daily Express

Miss Dorothy Provine, as she indicated but did not say, was clearly on the watch for secret agents following her and tapped telephones. She recalled a tale told her by pianist Rubinstein of one of his visits to Moscow. Mr Rubinstein, seeking for bugging in his hotel room, discovered some cunningly concealed wires under the carpet and carefully cut them all with his nail scissors, before going to bed.

'The next morning,' said Miss Provine, 'the chambermaid told him: "A funny thing happened last night. For no reason at all the chandelier in the room below fell down."'

Evening Standard

A kitten with two complete heads and three eyes has been born at Long Sutton.

* * * * * * * *

Mr G— of Long Sutton, a well known veterinary surgeon, has relinquished his practice to join the Church of England Ministry.

Sunday paper

SAN DIEGO, CALIFORNIA, DEC. 28. MRS R. S. WYGAL MAILED A FRUIT CAKE TO HER SON SGT. EDWARD R. W. RO MMMMM. MMMMM. MM. MMM. M MMMMM. MM. MMMM. MMM.... MMMMM..M...MMMMM.M.MMMM. MMMM... MMM..... M. MMMM. MMMMM. MMMM MM... MMMM... M. M. MMMMM. MMM. MMMM... M.MM. M MMMMM... M.MMMMM.

United Press Message

Miss Dorothy Morrison, who was injured by a fall from a horse last week, is in St Joseph's Hospital and covered sufficiently to see her friends.

Morristown (N.D.) News

I take back, with the greatest regret, the libellous remarks I made about Fräulein Anna Munkelbeck.

Clever Kreisblatt

Mr S— said he regarded himself as married to Miss B— as fair before God. He had not been previously married, but on the advice of friends obtained an affidavit that he was married and had two children to give to the income tax inspector.

Daily Telegraph

A woman dialled 999 last night when she was unable to get into an outside lavatory at a public-house because the lock was jammed. Police at Ashford, Kent, sent a sergeant to free the door.

A police spokesman said: 'To us it was just another emergency call. I think the lady felt the same way.'

Daily Mail

Father Antonio Corsi, a Capuchin friar, accused at Velletri, Italy, of cigarette smuggling, said yesterday that he thought he was handling macaroni. Had he known it was contraband he would have 'thrown it into the lake with my own hands'.

The Guardian

MODEL PLANE KILLS 4 COWS

A 14-year-old schoolboy's radio-controlled model aeroplane killed four pedigree cows worth over £500 when it got out of control and crashed.

Andrew Burton, who was flying the 4-foot plane from the wartime airfield at Hornchurch, Essex, found it would not respond. It climbed to over 500 feet and flew out of sight. When it ran out of petrol it crashed into a pylon on a farm five miles away and brought down an 11,000-volt power cable.

Nineteen cows were in the field at the time and four of them, grazing on marshy ground near the cable, were electrocuted. The accident cut off power to the farm and to part of the village of Rainham.

The Guardian

DOGS FOUND WORRYING
WILL BE SHOT

Notice in Henley-on-Thames park

A gale attaining a velocity of 72 miles an hour swept over New York last night. Humorous persons were injured by falling signs and bricks.

West Indian paper

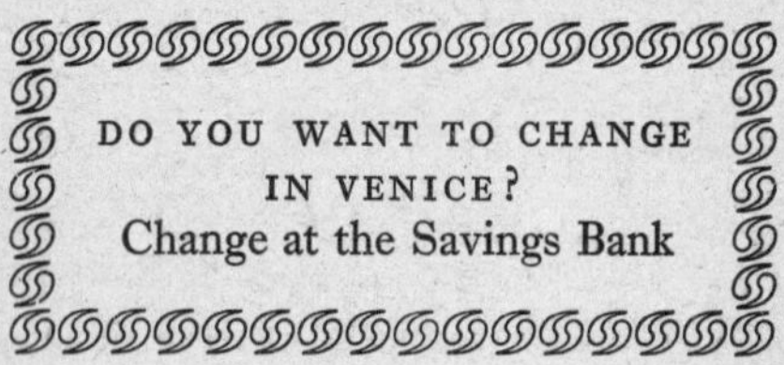
DO YOU WANT TO CHANGE IN VENICE?
Change at the Savings Bank

Venice leaflet

The fox made a bee-line through the Hall grounds, then on through the village, to the delight of the hundreds of spectators. Scent was lost in the fields that skirt the south side of the village, but a few moments later there were shouts in a garden near to the church, and within a few minutes the hounds had killed these scores of sightseers looking on from the surrounding gardens. It was one of the most exciting days we can remember.

Wilts paper

TWO WHIPPET PUPS FOR SALE, 9 ft × 9 ft 6 in, all fittings on skids.

Shropshire Journal

POLICE FOUND SAFE UNDER BLANKET

Headline in *Gloucestershire Echo*

The washerwomen of Venezuela smoke their cigarettes in reverse, with the hot ends inside their mouths. Harvard research workers have been studying the results of this novel smoking habit. They have noted that this form of smoking seems to ease toothache, and that no smokers show any symptoms of cancer, but they have to remember to flick off the ash whenever necessary.

The Guardian

A birthday party in observance of David Piatt's 17th birthday anniversary was given Friday evening in the home of Mrs Chester Piatt at 601 W. Vine St.

The birthday cake presented to David, who aspires to be a mortician, was in the shape of a coffin decorated in white and brown and colorful flowers.

Mount Vernon (*Ohio*) *News*

OUR WORKING SCHEDULE

Starting time	9.00 a.m.
Morning Coffee Break	9.30 - 11.30 a.m.
Lunch Hour	12.00 - 2.00 p.m.
Afternoon Tea Break	2.30 - 4.30 p.m.
Home Time	5.00 p.m.

Notice in National Lending Library, Boston Spa

Motorists say harsh things about insurance rates. But a driver in America recently ran off the road passing an airfield, collided with a hangar, caught fire, and burned out eleven aeroplanes.

Punch

CARLISLE's one-way traffic experiment, which brought vehicles in the city centre to a halt yesterday morning, achieved its object, claimed Mr L. J. A. Stow, the City surveyor and engineer.

Cumberland paper quoted in *Daily Telegraph*

The bride and bridegroom left for Italy, the latter wearing a hyacinth-blue hat of crinoline straw, and a blue velvet cloak over a dress of hyacinth-blue crêpe de Chine.

Essex paper

To taking up board to look
for smell and replacing same. 10s. 6d.

Plumber's bill

If the motion were passed, no strike action would be taken by NALGO without a ballet of all its members.

Bristol Evening Post

To test people's reaction to the bangs during yesterday's demonstration, Government scientists from the Ministry of Technology, the Building Research Laboratory and other bodies were scattered around the bang path, running from the Wash to Bedford.

Daily Mail

There have been times when I used to follow a lonely white-eye in the forest singing lustily all the time, hopping from tree to tree, as though calling for a mate.

American Cage-Bird Magazine

It is 'bitter only' for the donkey in the bar of the Vernon Young Arms at Croxton, near Stafford. Nobody objects when 'Clem', the three-year-old donkey, trots into the bar for his nightly pint. But it is no use offering him mild. For this donkey knows his ale and is strictly a bitter fan.

Mrs Audrey Sillitoe, wife of the licensee commented: 'One night the children brought him into the bar for a laugh. To our amazement we found he liked a drink of bitter. We have another donkey called Tina, but we don't allow her in as we feel we shouldn't encourage women to drink.'

Mrs Sillitoe added: 'Clem comes in the bar once or twice a week. I don't know of any brewery regulations which state that animals mustn't drink on the premises.'

Daily Express

A SAUSAGE FACTORY'S SAD STORY

A businessman who bought a neighbouring sausage skin factory, so that the smells attendant upon it should cease for good, has been told that its use must be confined to trades within the category of 'existing rights'.

These include the boiling of blood, the breeding of maggots, the manufacture of glue or manure, and, of course, the production of sausage skins. The businessman, Mr George Tebbutt, of Burnham Green Road, Welwyn, is, perhaps understandably, not anxious to venture personally into any of these commercial spheres. He is therefore advertising for a tenant.

Mr Tebbutt bought the factory a year ago, hoping to build a house on the site. Hertfordshire rural district council broke the news about green belt and 'existing rights' as gently as possible.

The Guardian

German Johann Vilberth, 32, saw his car being stolen, so he went to the local airport, hired a plane and flew round till he spotted the car miles away. Police arrested the thief.

The Sun

THIS IS THE GATE OF HEAVEN
ENTER YE ALL BY THIS DOOR

This door is kept locked because
of the draught

Seen at Cumberland church

The match was unfinished owing to measles. Craghurst was compelled to scratch.

The Harrovian

Connoisseurs only place tripe, feet, and condiments by layers in their brassière, first the carrots, then the tripe and pieces of beef.

Evening paper

(Readers should note in the above item Gobfrey Shrdlu's brilliant eye for visual effect.)

Mr Sparrow, secretary of the B— Company Ltd, has been granted six months leave of absence. Accompanied by Mrs Swallow he sailed on Saturday on a trip to Europe.

Australian paper

RELIABLE and experienced baby-sister
available. Ring 4572 after 4.30 p.m.

Advert in New Zealand paper

Keeping all food under cover is the first step towards ridding the house of aunts.

Albany Journal

A man who wanted a close-up photograph of an orang-utang at Auckland Zoo ended up by having his film eaten – by the orang-utang.

Disregarding a warning notice, the man climbed the protective railing that keeps the crowds a few feet from the orang-utang's cage, and lined up his camera. The orang-utang slowly extended its arms through the bars and suddenly grabbed the man, forcing him to the ground. The ape then started taking off the man's clothes as bystanders pelted it with buns and bags of peanuts.

This caused the animal to slacken its grip. Then it suddenly noticed the camera. Releasing the man, it took hold of the camera, twiddled the knobs, opened the back, and took out the film. Part of this it ate. The rest it festooned round its neck. The man vanished in the crowd.

Daily Mail

Sir, – Like the Rev. Eric James we also were constantly wiping our cat's paw-marks from the bonnet of our Morris Mini, until six weeks ago when we exchanged the mini for a Hillman Imp. The engine now being at the rear, the cat tried in vain to find her accustomed warm spot on the bonnet. It has not yet occurred to her to seek elsewhere. We hope it won't. – Yours faithfully,

Freda Boole (Mrs).
The Guardian

The other night my husband got up and, still asleep, apparently made a garden in the middle of our flat. After he had walked about in the dark for a while I heard him fill a cup with water. I told him to turn on the light, and asked him what he was doing. 'Planting bulbs,' he replied, turning on the light – and the radio.

Next morning there were straight lines of water all over the floor. Now I'm waiting for the flowers to come up.

Letter in *Daily Mirror*

Dip your soiled face in alcohol, rinse it in the liquid and hang it straight out to dry. It may then be pressed.

Toronto Mail

C— Society At Home
SEMI LADIES EVENING
on Thursday March 24th,
Dinner 6.30 Dancing

Invitation card

Among the side reactions of this mercurial drug the most important is the death of the patient shortly after the injection.

New York State Medical Journal

Mr J. Cox continued, saying a public health inspector visited the local dairy, where a dirty official admitted that the bottle was one of theirs.

Stratford-upon-Avon Herald

After the accident Mr Jones and his wife were treated for abrasions of the left hip and contusions of both arms. Mrs Platt was treated at General Hospital for a laceration of her right rear leg.

Philadelphia paper

FOR SALE Complete mahogany Chip & Dale dining-room set, in good condition, reasonable.

Advert in *Long Island Press*

Sir, – The fine article on the subject of self-employment of research chemists is most likely to provoke serious thought amongst those who are 'too old at forty', and the following case history which has come to my attention may interest readers.

A qualified chemist of many years' frustration had been given every encouragement short of dismissal by his employers to better his lot. With the proceeds of the sale of his home in the south, plus refunded pension-fund contributions, he secured suitable premises in an industrial area in the north-west.

In his roles as process operator, salesman, accountant and cleaner he was hard pressed to meet the increasing demands of his customers and had to train a member of the family to operate the hot-oil baths used for the final stage of the process. This enabled him to devote more of his time to dealing with customers, and extensions to the premises soon became necessary. He became financially very comfortable early in the venture, and attributed his success to insistence on rigorous standards of quality control. He is now considering opening a new plant and has toyed with the idea of mobile sales.

The chemist in this case was not a member of the Royal Institute of Chemistry, which is a pity, for the *Register* does not list any managing directors of high-class fish and chip restaurants.

W. T. Cuthbert, Urmston, Lancs.

Chemistry in Britain

Typists in an office block were getting electric shocks every time they touched a typewriter, electrical engineer Frank Booton told a supervisors' safety training course at Pfizer's factory in Sandwich, Kent. The cause was static build-up from walking on a nylon carpet, helped by a dry atmosphere.

A humidifier was introduced to dampen the air, but it was too effective. The girls' hair went straight. The office is now getting a smaller humidifier.

Universal News Service

It was not until the outcry after the robbery that the burglars knew they had made such a valuable haul. Then they were faced with the impossibility of selling their plunder.

WHY NOT SELL IT THROUGH A SMALL
ADVERTISEMENT IN THE HERALD?

Australian paper

MATINS

Hymn 43 'Great God, what do I see and hear?'
Preacher Rev. Dr Bernard Taylor.
Hymn 45 'Hark! an awful voice is sounding.'

Church notice-board

. . . and remember you can make a wonderfully nourishing broth from the remains if you have an invalid in the house.

Notice in butcher's

LABOUR M.P. SLAMS
CURB ON MIGRANTS

Headline in *The Sun*

THE FORD FOUNDATION announced today that it is giving $85 million (£30,356,000) to some 50 leading American symphony orchestras.

At a Press Conference today in New York Mr Henry Heald, the Foundation's president said one quarter of the grant would be on a no-strings basis.

Daily Telegraph

LEARN TO DRIVE
AS YOU WATCH TV

Headline in *The Sun*

RIGHT DOWN THE DRAIN

by John Davy, our Science Correspondent

With the help of the American National Science Foundation and the resources of the University of Sydney, five scientists have cleared up a matter of some importance to bathers all over the world.

They have shown conclusively that Australian bath water tends to rotate clockwise as it goes down the plughole.

It is now two and a half years since Mr Ascher H. Shapiro, of the Massachusetts Institute of Technology, showed in some classical experiments that his northern hemisphere bath water rotated *anti*-clockwise. But what would bath water do in the southern hemisphere?

There had been speculation – backed by sound physical reasoning – that bath water should reverse direction south of the equator. Indeed, keen observers on board cruise ships claimed to observe just this as they crossed from one hemisphere to the other. But now delicate tests in a cement-lined Sydney basement, with the temperature held constant at 20 deg. C., have confirmed theory by experiment.

Bath water experiments are not for amateurs. It appears, for example, that if the water swirls clockwise as it flows into the bath, it may still be swirling 18 hours later. The motion is imperceptible, but sufficient to upset experiments. So the Sydney team, using a circular 6-ft tub 9 in. deep, with a central plughole, left their bath water to settle for 18 hours before letting it out. They floated a cork delicately on the surface to show rotation – and when they pulled the plug a clockwise rotation developed consistently.

The Observer

A Hampshire friend reports that an entry in her eight-year-old son's diary has convinced her that strict discipline continues to be maintained in British boarding-schools. The entry reads: 'I must not clean my teeth with salad cream during prayers.'

Evening Standard

PARROT DISEASE FEARS

- - - - -

R.S.P.C.A. WILL ARRANGE PAINLESS END FOR OWNERS OF BIRDS

Essex paper

Miss Y—, the well-known singer, was nearly poisoned at one time. So she said at the meeting on Tuesday. When she stated that she had been nearly poisoned, the features of the members expressed regret.

Irish paper

In the handicrafts exhibition at Wordsley Community Centre, the contribution of the Misses Smith was 'smocking and rugs' and not 'smoking drugs' as stated in last week's report.

The County Express, Stourbridge

Unfortunately the Prime Minister had left before the debate began. Otherwise he would have heard some caustic comments on his absence.

Liverpool paper

The winter bride who closed the parade wore wool – but what wool – a dress of cobweb muslin, fan-pleated from breast to ahem.

Yorkshire Evening News

In the living-room Mr Wisegold of Wisegold and Wisegold was perspiring freely and photographing the bridal party in various combinations.

Surrey paper

Sir, – I dialled my friend Arthur Green and, to my surprise, got through instantaneously.

Is that you Arthur?
Yes, this is Arthur.
What time is our lunch today?
Lunch today? I don't understand.
You are Arthur Green, aren't you?
Yes, I'm Arthur Green.
Well, we've a lunch date in Town today.
Lunch date in Town? There must be some confusion.
You are Arthur Green of Toc H?
No, I'm Arthur Green the telephone engineer, and I'm mending your line.

Yours truly,
Rupert Bliss.
Letter in *The Times*

Sir, – Up in Holy Island, where we are filming *Cul-de-sac*, we noted with interest your editorial 'Yaks on Parade'. You did omit one use for yaks' hair that's pretty important to the entertainment industry: in small, almost 'powdered' form it is invaluable for reproducing unshaven stubble. We have been using this daily for two months on actors Lionel Stander and Jack MacGowran.

In case you wonder how this is applied, our make-up expert informs me that he uses a thin coating of embalmer's wax (because it does not glisten like ordinary adhesives), and then applies the small yak hairs, which even in the largest close-ups look exactly like unshaven stubble.

Multiply our film by all the other films, plays, TV productions and so forth, and it is obvious that the London Zoo should have all the encouragement possible in their yak breeding programme.

Sincerely, LILY POYSER,
Compton-Tekli Film Productions Ltd.,
60–62 Old Compton St, W.1

The Times

Maximum prices for all corsets and brassières have been revised. . . . This order also reduced the percentage uplift allowed to a manufacturer.

Board of Trade Journal

If it had not been for the United States Navy, the World War would have resulted in the real Agamemnon that so many predicted at the time.

U.S. Naval Air Station Bulletin

When deployed, section commanders were apt to shoot themselves instead of seeing that their men understood the Fire Orders.

O.T.C. report in school magazine

Asked his conception of the Navy's role in a future war, Morrison picked up his book. 'As certain as night succeeds the day, without a decisive navoin oiniou oiuiouiouoo ing definitive,' he read. 'Know who wrote that?'

Quincy (Mass.) *Patriot Ledger*

As from Monday, the catering assistants will serve customers to all potatoes.

Factory notice-board

Then with great courage, Mr Don Williams of the R.S.P.C.A. dropped over the wall into the alleyway as policeman held the wolf with noses tied to long sticks.

Manchester Evening News

BOLOGNA, December 13. *Umberto Montanari was unable to get rid of a mouse which chewed holes in his car's carpet, so he put a pot of water inside the vehicle and dropped a block of carbide into it. The method succeeded. An explosion destroyed the mouse – and the car.*

Reuter

A doctor examined a woman in Norfolk who complained of a pain under the upper plate of her false teeth, and found a tomato plant growing there.

Dr Patrick Luffman, of Burnham Market, says in the *British Medical Journal* that the pip was growing into the skin with roots $\frac{1}{16}$ to $\frac{1}{8}$ of an inch long.

Daily Mail

ALL TWISTED UP

A delinquent whelk

A 'left-handed' whelk – one whose shell spirals anti-clockwise – has been caught off Walton-on-the-Naze, by Mr Jonas Oxley, coxwain of Walton lifeboat.

Mr L. Sinsbury, a conchologist, said: 'No scientist knows why all the billions of whelks should spiral clockwise, but the catching of this left-handed whelk will throw many existing theories in the melting pot. A keen watch will be kept for other specimens, but as far as I am aware this shell is unique among modern freaks.'

The freak whelk was found when Mr Oxley's catch was being prepared for sale in his shop. It is now on display.

The Guardian

WIFE PLEADS FOR DELICATE WHALE

Headline in *Daily Express*

Sir Harry had his top lip caught under his lower teeth.

From a novel

Arrangements for teas were in the hands of Miss C—, the daughter of the Archdeacon and a lady member of the congregation.

Kent paper

WET CLEANER REQUIRED
FOR DRY CLEANERS

Advert in local paper

To the question 'In general do you approve or disapprove of Mr Johnson as President?' 72 per cent of those asked replied 'Yes' and 28 per cent 'No'.

Surrey paper

The new automatic couplings fitted to the organ will enable Mr S— to change his combinations without moving his feet.

Parish Magazine

Muncipal Judge Charles S. Peery, who performed the brief wedding ceremony, said plaintively: 'I forgot to kill the bride. And I'm sorry.'

Tarrytown News

Q. *How can I make use of left-over fruit juice?*
A. If a cup of fruit juice is left over, mix it with one cupful of sugar, two tablespoons of corn-starch, and the yolks of two eggs. It makes a delicious filling on kid shoes.

North Carolina paper

Sailors in the frigate Blackpool put a message in a rum bottle and dropped it into the Atlantic. It read: 'Finder is invited aboard for a tot of rum.'

Seven months later came the reply: 'Send the drink by post.' The bottle was found by Mr Donald Macisaac, 500 miles away at North Uist, Outer Hebrides. The men, who reached Portsmouth yesterday from the Far East, sent Mr Macisaac a bottle.

Daily Mail

BABY IAN MAKES HIS DAD A BANKER

Dad was having an afternoon nap yesterday when 12-months-old Ian Wilson climbed up on his knee. Ian burbled away as he examined 29-year-old Noel Wilson's half-open mouth. Then he popped in a half-crown, and pushed it well home with a finger.

Lorry driver Noel gulped, and woke up to find his son, the youngest of four children, smiling at him.

Last night, Mr Wilson, of Amberley Street, Sunderland, was in the town's Royal Infirmary. After being X-rayed, he was put on a diet and is being kept under observation to see whether an operation is necessary.

Said Mr Wilson: 'Ian's a little rip. While I was sleeping he had obviously taken me to be similar to a money box. He hasn't got a money box of his own, but it will be the first thing I buy him when I get out – with the same half-crown if we get it back.'

Daily Express

Filipino cabaret artist Glad Yates calls his act 'chamber music with a difference'. He beats drumsticks on chamberpots.

Tit-Bits

Complete home for sale; two double, one single bed, dining-room threepiece suite, wireless, television, carpets, lion, etc.

Advert in *Portsmouth Evening News*

Mrs George was married before anaesthetics came into use in surgical operations.

Ludlow (*Indiana*) *Tribune*

'Aqui estamos y aqui nos quedaremos,' fueron las palabras dichas por Sir Alec Douglas Hyphen Home.

Argentine paper

The hospital extension will enable patients to be prepared and served in a way that has not been possible in the past.

Lancs paper

A son was born to Mr and Mrs William Kleintop, Lehigh Avenue, during the past week. Congratulations, Pete!

Palmerton (*Pennsylvania*) *Press*

Driving tuition. More pupils wanted. 10s. per lesson; asses every week.

Cumberland Evening News

The competitors from Limerick are so large that a special train is to be run.

Irish paper

Morning exercise for Ted Matson of Portland, Oregon, is a ping-pong match with Dagwood, his cat. Dagwood, using his paw for a paddle, has a game each morning before breakfast with his master. Matson wins just a little better than half the games. In one exchange Dagwood returned the ball fifteen times.

Amazing but True by Doug Storer

FABULOUS BALLAST

The U.S.S. *Trout* received orders to proceed to Corregidor with a cargo of badly needed medical supplies. To accomplish its mission it was necessary to unload all of her torpedoes and all other heavy equipment that could be spared. The *Trout* made Corregidor and spent three days unloading her cargo under fire from Japanese batteries on Bataan. In order to slip out past the enemy, the sub had to have a heavy ballast for a quick descent. The diving officer wanted bags of gravel, but they were needed for breastworks on Corregidor, shortly to be under siege.

An Army officer suggested money be used for ballast. Ten million dollars' worth of gold bars belonging to the Philippine Commonwealth, banks, mines and residents of Corregidor were loaded on to the *Trout*. The sub slipped past the enemy and transferred its fabulous ballast to a cruiser.

Amazing but True by Doug Storer

A MARBLE STATUE almost 28 feet high has been erected in Canden, Maine, U.S.A. It is in memory of Capt. Hanson Gregory who perfected the technique of making the hole in the doughnut – in 1847.

News of the World

Wrap poison bottles in sandpaper and fasten with scotch tape or a rubber band. If there are children in the house, lock them in a small metal box.

Philadelphia Record

Recent tests conducted by a zoologist proves that grasshoppers hear with their legs. In all cases the insects hopped when a tuning fork was sounded nearby. There was no reaction to this stimulus, however, when the insects' legs had been removed.

Corning Glass Works Magazine

The Post Office sought permission to erect telephone poles on the Llanfoist housing site. They have been told that whilst the Council do not object to the installation of telephones, they consider the poles should be laid underground.

Abergavenny Chronicle

Mr Selwyn Lloyd has mobilized forces in his hand and plans to break the oil bottleneck up his sleeve.

Daily Telegraph

The husband's allegation of cruelty was rejected, but the judge exercised discretion in respect of his own misconduct.

Daily Mail

The flame will burn for 16 days and nights until the closing ceremony on December 8. It is fed by cylinders of profane gas.

Bristol Evening Post

The most unusual use of ultrasonics occurred recently in a motion picture theatre. The theatre transmitted low-frequency sounds during the intermission of the matineé and early evening performances in an attempt to clear the theatre of youngsters seeing the film a second time round.

These low-frequency sounds create, in most individuals, a feeling of uneasiness and fear. Everyone left the cinema.

Reveille

DOG MUST CUT DOWN SMOKING

Moustique, the dog was sulking in her kennel today. For she has been ordered to cut down on her smoking. Instead of her daily nine pipes of tobacco, Moustique has been limited to two.

Moustique started smoking nine months ago. Her owner, Mme. Jeanne Bichez of Marq, near Calais, saw that she was always chewing pieces of wood, so she offered her son's pipe to her pet. Moustique loved it – filled and lit. Soon she was smoking two or three ounces of tobacco a week.

But a month ago Mme. Bichez noticed that her pet's eyes were puffed. The vet was called. His diagnosis: Moustique must cut down drastically – or go blind.

Daily Mirror

Dr O. Nacke, 48 Bielefeld, Stapenhorststrasse 62, Germany, asks for references for a collection of pictures on the work of the librarian and documentationist – representations of all times and all spheres of work of these two professions, including electronic data processing. Senders of pictures which have been accepted will receive as a token of gratitude a nice etching by the woman painter Clara Ernst showing the flood of literature and how it is mastered by documents and libraries.

The Assistant Librarian

At the fair they will be exhibiting a full range of shoes for girls with low-cut fancy uppers.

Leicester Mercury

To brighten gold braid, give it a cake, put it whole into a steamer and steam for 20 minutes; it will then be thoroughly warm. Split in two toast and butter well.

Brooklyn Daily Times

BIRTHS. In Sherburne, October 6, a son, 10 pounds, Frederick Albert, to Mr and Mrs Russell L. and Nancy (Johnson) Stocker.

Vermont Standard

'But we do not want a repetition of the farce that occurred on the last occasion we saw the Board,' he said, 'when a lot of sand was thrown in our eyes. This time we want something more concrete.'

Fulham Chronicle

NOTICE

Any persons passing beyond
this point will be drowned

BY ORDER OF THE MAGISTRATES

Sign in Essex

WANTED – Wet fish or experienced man or woman to take charge of business.

Advert in *Bristol Evening Post*

One day 18-year-old university student Ron Richards, of Wolfville, Nova Scotia, started brushing his teeth and kept on . . . and on . . . and on – for 31 hours, 31 minutes, and 31 seconds. When it was over and he was asked if there was anything he wanted, he replied: 'A new toothbrush.'

Weekend

When my husband reads in bed on warm nights he puts a colander over his head. He says it keeps off the flies, shades his eyes from the light and lets in air at the same time – Mrs L. Taylor, Bradford.

C.W.S. *Good Shopping*

Dr Thrush, an expert on typhoid fever, remarked in the course of his evidence that he had swallowed millions of typhoid bacilli.

Mr Justice Lawrence: How did you like them?

Dr Thrush: The thing occurred accidentally. I was testing water which was said to contain typhoid bacilli. The weather was hot and I swallowed a glass of water, and then discovered I had drunk the water in which I had put the typhoid germs. For three weeks I enjoyed the pleasures of imagination, and when the three weeks had passed and nothing had happened I felt happy.

Daily Mail

Half of 48-year-old Alfredo Rontardo's house is in Venezuela, and half in Colombia. He could hardly have it better. He is wanted by police for an offence punishable only in Venezuela. Whenever they come to arrest him, he just nips into his bedroom. That's in Colombia.

Weekend

If you have a sack that is full of holes don't throw it away, empty them out into a clean box and store in the dry; they may be useful when you start bulb planting.

Reading Horticultural Corporation's *Garden Topics*

It was felt by the Luncheon Club Committee that although Crême Caramel was on the menu more frequently after the previous meeting, it had tended to drop off recently.

Factory bulletin

LABOUR M.P. COLLAPSES
IN COMMONS

Sitting suspended as he is
carried out on stretcher

Northern paper

LOST, one four-poster brass pyramid with Terylene mudguards and retractable plastic legs; reward.

Bristol Evening Post

LOST – almost all white cat.

Bury Times

If you are willing to pay just a little more and are looking for a really fascinating, out-of-the-ordinary pet, may we suggest you try the second floor and ask to see our Miss Martimore.

Sign in Toronto store, quoted in *Daily Mirror*

GOAT required on loan, September. London; exceptional specimen; house trained; odourless; nanny or billy. Telephone WHI 5957.

Advert in *The Times*

JUDGE GORDON WINBORN refused to see the evidence in a case at Louisville, Kentucky, today. Kelly Clemon, 51, was charged with using a reptile when he was speaking at a church service.

He wanted to produce the evidence – a six-foot rattlesnake with six rattles. 'Not in my court,' said the judge. 'You can put me down as a coward.' The case was adjourned.

Daily Express

The signature on the £10 cheque looked familiar, but Mrs Joseph Broussard, of Houston, Texas, couldn't remember making it out, as she was ticking off the cheques returned with her bank statement. So the bank looked into it – and they found there was another Mrs Joseph Broussard on their books. The two Mrs Broussards not only have almost identical signatures, but both are five-feet-two-inches tall, weigh the same, and both had the same doctor.

When they compared notes about their husbands, they found that both Joseph Broussards had come from New Iberia, Louisiana, both have dark brown hair and both drive 1956 cars of the same make and colour. One Joseph Broussard, however, is three years younger, two inches shorter, and 20 lbs heavier than the other Joseph.

Weekend

WANTED: Man to work on nuclear fissionable isotope molecular reactive counters and three-phase cyclotronic uranium photo synthesizers No experience necessary.

Advert in *The Mines Magazine*

Capt. Lindholm and other officers emphasized that women should call police if they are accosted, or if they think they see or hear a prowler.

'We'll be there the next night,' he asserted.

Los Angeles Times

PRECAST CONCRETE FOREMEN
required in Hampshire

Advert in *Evening News*

The bride, who was given away by her father, wore a dress of white figured brocade with a trailing veil held in place by a coronet of pearls. She carried a bouquet of rose buds and goods vehicles, leaving free access to all private vehicles not built for more than seven passengers.

Atherstone News and Herald

On July 11 he suffered a stroke but with the loving care of his family and his efficient nurse, he never fully recovered.

Wisconsin paper

Sprinkle on the shelves a mixture of half borax and half sugar. This will poison every aunt that finds it.

Norwick (*Connecticut*) *Bulletin*

I am also told that a gents' toilet is to be built adjacent to the sub-station. If the local inhabitants of this part of Childwall stand for this they will stand for anything.

Letter in *Liverpool Echo*

While the Russians perfect the technique of 'disinformation', at least one television dealer in London is experimenting with a process called de-repairing. Submitting an estimate for putting right a TV set he explained that in fact the work had already been done: they had to do it, he said, to find out what the cost of doing it would be. The customer could if he wished refuse the estimate and in this case the engineers would be instructed to re-repair it and restore it to its original unsatisfactory state. There would however be an 'estimate charge' of 25s. to cover the cost of the exercise.

The Guardian

Izzy Lehmann, a tailor who loves gambling, ran out of cash during a poker game, so he wagered a new suit on the last hand. He lost to the man who had been winning all evening.

Back in his tailor's shop in Tel Aviv, Israel, Izzy kept his word and made the suit – but he put 18 pockets in it. He told the winner they were to hold his winnings. Two Italian firms heard about the suit and paid Izzy for his ideas and style.

The Sun

TOO MUCH HAIR ON HIS CHEST JOB REFUSED

A former Regular Army sergeant, Mr Alan Campbell, claimed yesterday that he was refused a job as a machine operative with an engineering firm at Cwmbran, in Monmouthshire, because he had too much hair on his chest.

'I've heard that it may be connected with abrasive oils getting into the hair but I worked previously as a machine operative and didn't have any trouble,' said Mr Campbell, aged 27, of York Place, Newport.

The Guardian

DOG BAN: MATRON TURNS DOWN POST

Glasgow Evening Citizen

We must keep our ears to the ground if we want to keep our heads above water.

B.B.C. Farm programme

FOLIES PARISIENNE

SEE! NUDES IN THE WATERFALL

DARING FAN DANCE. VIRGIN AND THE DEVIL

Sensational dance of the Strip Apache
Les Beaux Mannequins de Parisienne
Continental and Oriental Nudes
Old Age Pensioners Monday

Advert in Leicester paper

Honeymoons, from now onwards £5 5s.; quiet and central; hot and cold; separate tables.

Advert in *Aberdeen Press & Journal*

To serve, dip moulds in water to loosen the contents and serve with passion fruit and cream. British housewives can substitute pineapple, cherries or apricots for passion.

Romford Recorder

P.C. Roberts said he found the horse straying riding the bicycle. Noticing he was swaying a good deal, and that he had no trouser clips on, witness stopped him and questioned him about the cycle.

Kent paper

CURRY EATING SPECIALIST IS FINED £5

A stranger in an Indian restaurant in Southend tried to demonstrate to Mr Arthur Flint how he should eat his curried chicken and rice. Mr Flint demonstrated his displeasure by pushing the curry in his face. In return, Mr Flint received a blow on the head with a chair.

At Southend court today the stranger, William Parkins, aged 28, a paint colour matcher, of Boston Avenue, Southend, pleaded guilty to assaulting Mr Flint and was fined £5 with £3 3s. costs. Mr R. A. Shorter, prosecuting, said Mr Flint and a friend had ordered a meal when Parkins, sitting at a nearby table, spoke to them. He sat down uninvited and advised Mr Flint to drink a glass of water before eating the curry. Then he said he would show him how to prepare the meal, picked up the rice and poured it on the curry, and mixed it together. Mr Flint sat watching and then asked: 'Have you finished?' Mr Parkins said he had, whereupon Mr Flint picked up the plate and pushed it into his face.

The curry and rice ran down Parkins's clothing and following an argument, he left. Later, as Mr Flint sat eating a replaced meal, he felt a severe blow on the head and shoulders and on grappling with his assailant, found he had caught hold of the curry-stained Parkins. Police were called and Parkins told them: 'I hit him with a chair. My pride couldn't take it. He pushed me too far.'

In a statement he explained that he was only showing Mr Flint how to prepare his meal and added: 'He picked up the plate and pushed the whole lot in my face. I was shocked beyond belief because he seemed so friendly.'

Evening Standard

Rusty, a pony owned by a 16-year-old grammar school girl, Elizabeth Millbank, of East Street, Blandford, Dorset, is terrified by fireworks. So on the 5th November she will sit with him and read Shakespeare aloud.

Daily Mail

Order your nuts NOW. If you have any difficulty, drop me a envelope addressed to yourself and marked 'Nuts'.

Gardening column in *Reveille*

Within a year from his return he had both married and observed the comet which bears his name.

New Scientist

Heaven had allowed me no time to be anything but a happy June bride. Simon afterwards told me that I looked cheerful, expectant, and serene as I came up the aisle.

Woman

It was agreed that existing counter and writing supervising officers, both men and women, should immediately be liable to rotate on posts which had hitherto been reserved to the other sex.

Post

It was a mistake about Hermann, and the boys at Texas Christian University named their horned frog mascot Hermannia after finding nine baby frogs in the pen, have apologized. Father consisted of spaghetti, peppers, whisky and coffee.

Washington paper quoted in '*Bloomers*' by John Audrey

SPRING FLOWER AND EGG SERVICE

Address by Rev. Edwin Strange

Parents and adult fiends are especially invited

Waveney Chronicle

A man I know who wants to remain anonymous until he has finished his thesis has been tagging sexton beetles on Hampstead Heath in an effort to find out how long it takes a hare's head to disintegrate. There is more to this ecological exercise than meets the eye, for the rate of disappearance of carrion affects arguments about the observable effects of, for example, pesticides on wild life. The investigator cadged a liberal supply of hares' heads from a West End hotel and buried them at approximately hundred yard intervals in a transect stretching from Parliament Hill to Highgate Heights.

After a few days he nobbled about forty sexton beetles – those black and red burrowers into carrion; he daubed them with luminous nail varnish and released them again about a mile away to see if they returned to their egg-sustaining pits of putrescence. They did, but also triggered off an unenvisaged socio-ecological cycle. Four beetle-bournes on the south flank of Kenwood attracted such a variety of local curs that irate adolescents took to throwing sods at them; they were interfering with their courtship.

By the time one or two keepers had restored the peace, a statistically significant number of baits had been carried off by Hampstead poodles with an apparent beetle deficiency. The experiment shows that carrion does indeed disappear quickly and unpredictably. The next step might be to peg out a few chemical manufacturers on Wimbledon Common and see what happens to them.

New Scientist

Approximately 300,000 American men are now wearing hairpieces, but manufacturers think this is just scratching the top of the market. Only two out of ten men reach 35 with a full head of hair. Of the remaining eight unfortunates, three will have no hair on top, three will be in intermediate stage (severe hairline recession or bald patches) and two will be 'covering' private evidence not yet noticeable to others.

News Front (U.S.A.)

The number of thefts of locks, especially locks of shops, in Dessuk, Lower Egypt, has increased considerably during the past few days.

The police believe that a gang specializing in lock thefts is responsible.

Egyptian paper

Will parishes who so far have made no payment do so without fail before the end of the year and so save my grey hairs. There are 68 of them at the time of writing.

Diocesan Magazine

BLUTHNER pianist wanted, upright and grand.

Advert in Yorks paper

Surely the parents and school teachers are to blame here. You find them playing both on the main and by-pass roads, throwing each other's caps and dashing out after them, and many similar games.

Letter in Ealing paper

287 – The Shepherd's Guide: this book is a practical treatise on diseases of sheep . . . Edinburgh 1807, 8vo, half sheep, worn, uncut, slight worm.

Booksellers' catalogue

Hand your luggage to us
WE WILL SEND IT IN ALL DIRECTIONS

Advert of Tokyo forwarding agency

Some years ago I witnessed a classic example of the results of haste in design. That well-known agricultural device the muck-spreader was being designed and my colleague had been bounced into doing the rather complex gear train design in record time. His protests that this work required an independent check were shouted down. 'No time,' they cried, 'issue the drawings at once and get on with the next part of the job!'

The prototype building went on apace and then came the day for the field demonstration. It was a nice day and the sun shone on the machine and the little group of people composed of customers' representatives and design staff who gathered round expectantly as the muck was loaded up and the operator took his seat. With spreader disengaged the vehicle moved forward, approaching the group slowly.

The operator's hand was seen to pull the spreader lever and then an extraordinary thing happened. A torrent of muck poured over the poor operator blotting him from view, and for good measure this unwelcome rain descended over the spectators with a vigour which was only matched by the strength of the accompanying odour. As my colleague said after he had taken up his new post: 'There were quite a number of places in the gear train where a left-hand helix angle instead of a right-handed one would have made a deal of difference to the success of the demonstration.'

Design in Industry

Unclaimed articles found in Naples streets during the year included: a farm tractor, two donkeys, a gravestone, two double beds, an ice-cream maker, a bath, a suitcase full of faded love letters – and 17 pairs of trousers.

News of the World

KING DENIES HE ATE 6 PEOPLE

Headline in *The Guardian*

Miss Ruby Yates suddenly reveals a delicious sense of comedy, and is quite irresistible in black pyjamas, over her kidneys and bacon.

Provincial paper

It is often said these days that it takes longer to traverse an ocean than it does to get to the office. Let us hope that by this scheme we shall reverse that trend.

Daily Telegraph

There may still be a few of these people around who think that the short-cut to social eminence is to be able to say: 'I'm a Conservative', but they come down the social ladder a rung or two when it can be seen that the blue rosette is being used to cover their threadbare trouser seats.

Letter in *Chingford Guardian*

The bottleneck in the brewery business is not so much in the bottled beer department as in the barrel department.

Evening Standard

Chess is a game of skill, played by two four smaller squares of equal size, coloured persons on a square board divided into sixty – alternately light and dark.

Book on chess

Cycling along a route used by Livingstone when he first saw Lake Tanganyika, a leopard suddenly leaped out of the forest in front of her.

Yorks paper

For 30 years the two old friends met for supper every night. And for 30 years John Quartero, now passed 70, bottled up his anger. The trouble: his friend Joe Cocito made the ravioli sauce too hot – and as the years slipped by old Joe made it hotter and hotter.

Last night Quartero could take no more. Without a word he stood up and left. This morning they met in the street and chef Joe asked John why he had walked out. John's reply was dramatic. He whipped out a gun and shot his friend in the leg.

Accused of assault with a deadly weapon, old John tearfully told Miami police: 'I couldn't stand Joe's hot sauce any longer.'

Daily Express

Asked if he had any of the stolen articles, the accused, James Smithers, replied: 'Yes, I have some of them at home and if you come and go with me now, I will give you them.'

Constable Weston said that at his home at Gilkes Land, Hindesbury Road, Smithers gave him a multi-coloured bath robe, seven shirts, three pairs of pants, two pairs of socks, one pouch of Ivorol, one shaving set, one pair of earrings, one window blind, one United States 5-cent piece, one torch light, and said 'These are all the things I get from Mrs Cox.'

The offence was alleged to be committed in January this year. Mrs Cox said she discovered certain articles missing when she was looking for the eighth, ninth and tenth books of Moses.

Barbados Advocate

Police patrolling Station Road, Oban, at one o'clock in the morning caught two men tying a 4½-ft long basking shark to a lamp-post with a grappling hook and a rope. Police ordered the men to untie the fish and take it to the police station.

Glasgow Bulletin quoted in *New Statesman*

The major event on the programme was the selection of a 'Queen of Spring', and late in the evening the parade of 'expectant queens' was a magnificent spectacle.

Tyrone Constitution

WOMAN REQUIRED
for looking over
fixed bats and cranks
in warehouse

Advert in *Staffordshire Evening Standard*

She picked up a snapshot of a dear friend who had recently died on her bedroom mantelpiece.

Quoted in '*Bloomers*' by John Audrey

Despite a temporary bitch in the opening chorus of the second act, Mr Jones earned high praise for his skilful stage management.

Review of '*The Gondoliers*'

About 40 immigrants for herd-testing work, three of them women, arrived in the Atlantis yesterday morning. They will be posted to various parts of the country. The three women all have an agricultural background and are looking forward keenly to their new opportunities. Miss Hornimant is a B.A. (Oxen).

New Zealand paper

WANTED – Part-time hotel receptionist and telephone operator (small broad). Apply – Hotel, Nicosia.

The Cyprus Mail

Even in the flea-circus times have changed. I talked to flea impressario Alfred Testo. 'We used to get fleas from crane-drivers' socks in a Hartlepool steel works,' he said. 'Now with all these disinfectants about, we have to advertise for them in the papers.'

Evening Standard

NEW YORK, Tuesday. Posing nude in the middle of the Manhattan financial district is no offence if the public is not watching, a Criminal Court judge ruled yesterday.

The 'public' was not taken to include a detective who arrested model Jan Tice, 27, as she stood unclothed at the corner of Broadway and Liberty Street. Also picked up were her companions: John Wilcock, 36, a free-lance writer, and Eugenie Lewis, 36, a photographer.

The three said they were preparing a book on the city's public sights. Jan, in the nude, was to figure prominently in the foreground of each scene. Detective Joseph Leary arrested all three, and they were accused of disturbing the peace. The trial was last month.

Judge Daly's decision was disclosed yesterday. 'Actually the defendants annoyed no one, interfered with no one, obstructed no one, except perhaps the police officer,' he said. 'A breach of the peace requires the presence of the public. The public relates to people. There weren't any people there.'

Evening Standard

A split meeting of the YFC was held on Monday night, when the boys learned a great deal from a talk on artificial insemination by a representative of the Southbar Cattle Breeding Centre. The girls learned much about the arrangement of flowers from Miss Moira Grant, Busby, who demonstrated the art. After tea, the boys continued with their talk while the girls examined the floral arrangements more closely.

Hamilton Advertiser quoted in *New Statesman*

Newry Council refuses to buy a new piano for dancers at the town hall, because the present one smokes too much and drinks too much stout.

Sunday Express

The theory of the latest electronic computors was explained by Mr H. B. La Costa when he lectured to Hull and District Society of Incorporated Secretaries. He said that not only would a computor fiXnd an error, but would cor restit and continue to perform without a pause in contuity.

Daily Mail

(Note that Gobfrey Shrdlu intervenes where he knows the shoe will pinch most.)

Mrs Perkins had pleaded guilty to obtaining and possessing a total of 40 oz. of opium and other drugs (18,000 dozes).

Glasgow paper

The Rev. Dr Charles Brown's career has been a striking one. He started life at the age of eight. . . .

Oxford paper

The bride was attended by two bridesmaids. Both were nearly attired in dresses of fawn georgette.

Lincolnshire paper

Miss Bates, well known artistic photographer, has had many celebrities amongst her patrons, and in 1956 she was awarded a good meal for her excellent work.

Shanghai paper

Suetonius, in Galba, cap. 6, Seneca, in his 81st Epistle, and Pliny, lib. 8 cap. 2, make mention of elephants that were taught to walk the rope (query, cable?) and this they did, both forwards and backwards, as well as up and down; and this feat Galba first caused to be exhibited to the Roman people. After this, such was the confidence reposed in the dexterity of the animal, that *a person sat upon an elephant's back while he walked across the theatre upon a rope, extended from the one side to the other!* Lipsius, who has collected these testimonies, thinks they are so strong that they cannot be doubted.

Scalinger (p. 728) says that elephants have been not only taught to dance upon the earth, but also upon the rope! Busbequius *saw* an elephant dance a *pas seul* at Constantinople. Elian says he saw one of these animals writing Roman letters with his trunk. In the reign of Tiberius, twelve elephants, six male and six female, were clothed like men and women, and performed a country dance; at length they went to a feast, where they ate and drank as men do, being great mimics.

The Recreative Review, 1821

BROKEN HILL, Australia, Thursday. Mr Allan Carmichael, 49, a farmer, was fined at Broken Hill today for driving a motor vehicle – an airplane – on a public highway under the influence of drink.

Constable W. Strachen told the magistrate's court that he saw Carmichael flying his Cessna airplane so low over the town of Ivanhoe he could see what he was wearing. He drove to the airport to interview the pilot, but on the way he met Carmichael, still in his airplane, driving along the road. He tried to get his police car out of the way, but even so the right wing-tip of the airplane hit the car.

Carmichael continued into Ivanhoe and pulled his airplane up outside the police station. He was seen to stumble and hold on to the airplane as he alighted. Mr Carmichael told the court he had hit a bull while driving along the road and had gone into town to report the incident. He had his flying licence suspended for seven days and was fined £A50 (£40).

News Agency

A motorcyclist was thrown off his machine in Edinburgh yesterday while attempting to pass a bus. The machine skidded on to the tram – of his own works including a sonata in the style of Handel.

Scottish paper

WANTED, Girls experienced, for
sticking up on toothpicks.
Apply B. & F. Pearlizing Co.

Advert in *Providence Evening Bulletin*

Two Ford cars were travelling behind each other in the direction of Liverpool.

Liverpool paper

GREAT MATCH IN NAIROBI. Thika put on a spurt during which Ritchie failed with a good attempt in the progeny. There are few things more hereditary than under-shot and swine-mouths, also soft and fluffy coats.

East African paper

WANTED, A1 male waitress. Don't answer unless qualified.

Advert in *Dallas News*

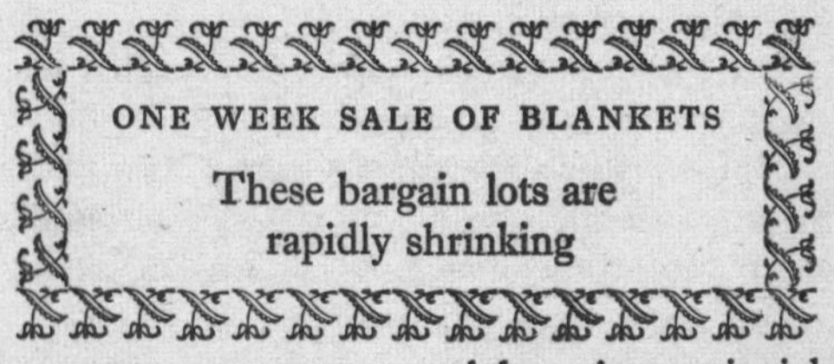

Advert in provincial paper

MIDWIFE, part-time, night club.

Advert in Irish paper

The body of Mrs Helen James, aged 30, was found yesterday, in a suitcase in a shed at her home in Elstead Avenue, Wembley Park. Police are satisfied there is no question of foul play. An inquest will be held at Hendon on Monday.

The Guardian

Sir, – Your delightful fifth leader on March 17 on an order for 10 million Beatles' records made of toffee prompts me to tell you that edible records are not new. As far back as 1903, British Patent No. 1992 was granted for such a product, which in fact was marketed. Novelty chocolate records, too, have been issued in more recent years. Certainly I know of a number of records I'd rather eat than play.

Yours faithfully, DONALD ALDOUS,
Technical Editor, *Audio and Record Review.*

The Times

We once heard of a traveller who told a story of an immense pie – so large, indeed, that after the crust and meat were eaten, a dozen couples danced in the dish, and one of them lost a buckle in the gravy. Now we cannot boast that Sheffield has ever produced such a pie, but one was exhibited and eaten at Mr Turner's on Christmas Eve, of the following size – one yard and a half long, two feet wide, one foot deep, ten feet round. It was baked by Mr Barlow, quite perfect; the crust consisting of six stone of rye meal.

New England Farmer, 1824

Two women were robbed of their handbags and one was punched in the South End district yesterday.

Boston Post

The Ballet travels with its own symphony orchestra which is directed by Mrs Goberman. The orchestra contains 20 virtous performers.

Clemson College Tiger

By going on one of our luxury cruises you will shorten the depressing winter months for others as well as yourself.

Shipping Company's leaflet

Gents 3-speed bicycle, also two ladies for sale, in good running order.

Lancashire paper

A high point of the affair was when Mrs Storace, Mrs Crossman, and Mrs Freeman performed a beach ballet for other members of the party during which Mrs Crossman broke three toes.

Long Island paper

Miss June Brown was a week-end guest at the Louis Scholl home. Mrs Louis Scholl was also a guest at the same home.

Ashland (Ohio) Times-Gazette

When the results were announced, aunts were thrown across the House and there were cries of 'Resign'.

Report in local paper

BUSINESSMAN Henri Bidard goes to sleep each night in a coffin in his garden. Henri, who is 53, explained at his home near Argentan, France: 'After we die, most of us are destined to spend the rest of eternity inside a coffin. I wanted to get accustomed to being inside one BEFORE I die.'

Sunday Mirror

HOT-CROSS BUNS 160 YEARS OLD

Hot-cross buns over one hundred and sixty years old are still in good condition in a London public house – the Widow's Son Inn in East London.

A widowed mother who kept the inn at the beginning of the last century used to put aside a hot-cross bun for her sailor son if he was at sea on Good Friday. One year he did not return. But the custom continued.

Reveille

The Ulster Bank, Killeshandra, Co. Cavan, was full of customers yesterday morning when a hawk flew through the window. The hawk dived into a heap of currency notes on the counter and flew towards the open door with a five-pound note in its beak.

Mr Tom McConville, cashier, leaped up on the counter and threw a paperweight at the bird which he felled. He rescued the five-pound note, escaping with a cut across the eye from the claws of the hawk.

Sunday Independent quoted in *Wide World*

HUSBAND STAMPED ON MAN WHO SENT LOVE LETTERS TO HIS LANDLADY

Headline in *Kent Messenger*

The Conference is still sitting, but hithertoo there has been no sign of that firm resolution on the part of the Australian Government to cut their throats according to the cloth, which alone can restore public confidence.

Australian paper

A postcard sent to the address on page 15 secures a week's supply of dental cream free. Get variety into your cooking.

Essex paper

In many parts of Co. Sligo hares are now practically unknown because of the unreasonable laughter to which they have been subjected in recent years.

Sligo paper

Deryk stood watching her, his hands in his pockets, a splendid specimen of English manhood in his white flannels, his tennis racket in his strong brown hands.

Story in church paper

Miss Miss Gladys Harrison (Contralto).

Notts paper

Charles Barer was fined 15s. for keeping a dog without a front light in Hawley Rd., Wilmington.

Kent paper

Our charges are commensurate to quality and can safely be assumed to be the lowest in the district.

Notice in Derby shop

A curious circumſtance happened a ſhort since, near a village not far from Malton in York Shire. A Chimney-ſweeper, in his way over a paſture, was attacked by a bull, and to ſave himſelf from the fury of the enraged animal, climbed into a tree, where he continued all night, and the Bull stood centinel at the bottom.

About four the next morning, a neighbouring Butcher, who was passing over the ſame field, drew the attention of the beast from his ſable friend, whom he immediately deſſerted, and began a freſh contest with the Butcher, who was obliged to make his eſcape by aſcending the tree already occupied (though unknown to him) by the Chimney-ſweeper. But what was his ſurprise, when, as he mounted the tree, he was accoſted by the man of Soot, with 'Good morning to you, Sir!' In this dilemma he was totally at a loſs what to do; he had just eſcaped from the Bull, and was now fallen (as he ſuppoſed) into the claws of the devil! whom, probably, from conſcientious motives, he dreaded ten times more than his adverſary below.

Such a situation was too much for human nature to ſupport; and he certainly had thrown himſelf down to the mercy of the Bull, had not the Sweep relieved his panic, by proving himſelf to be only a fellow-creature in the ſame predicament.

The Cabinet of Curiosities, 1810

MARRIAGE

In Kingston, N.H., Col. William Webster, aged 67, to Miss Martha Winslow, aged 19.

By the above union the bridegroom has married his sister's granddaughter, which makes the bride a wife to her great-uncle, sister to her grandfather and grandmother, aunt to her father and mother, and great-aunt to her brother and sister. She is stepmother to five children and one great-grandchild.

Curiosities of Matrimony, 1889

Would any lady give a large pram for the triplets recently born in the Liverpool Maternity Hospital.

Liverpool Daily Post

SISTERS WED BROTHERS
HAVE BABIES SAME DAY

New York Herald Tribune

Notice is given that after this date owners of any fowls on land tenanted by Mr Roger Manning, Hill Farm, will be destroyed.

Dorset paper

THIS IS A GENUINE OFFER – No connection with any other firm who are selling rubbish.

From a circular

The skirt was long and fluted, and fell to her ankles where it joined a simple bodice.

Hants paper

There are also the universities, in which it is estimated that one person in 1150 is educated.

Northumberland paper

The accident occurred on the bend of No. 16 platform while the driver of the stationary train was takin gin water.

Manchester paper

PIECE OF EAR LOST, FOUND, AND SEWN ON

A soldier, who had a third of his ear bitten off in a fight, had the missing piece sewn on again in hospital after a frantic search for it.

Fusilier James Doran, aged 22, of the Royal Highland Fusiliers, was rushed to the Cambridge military hospital at Aldershot, where his loss was discovered. The surgeon, Major G. Ellis, said he would restore the ear if the missing part could be found.

An ambulance carrying a duty corporal returned to the town centre where the fight had taken place, while Fusilier Doran stayed behind laughing and joking with doctors and staff. The missing piece was found under a stationary taxi within half an hour. Last night an Army spokesman said it was 'touch and go' whether the operation would be a success.

The Guardian

PEPPER AND COOK
THE JUDGES
IN RHODES CASE

Headline in *The Sun*

Witness said that on Christmas Eve Mrs Smith left Mr Smith alone like a dog, with only his pyjamas.

News Chronicle

Said Mr Justice Vaisey: 'It is a fearful thing to contemplate that, when you are driving along the road, a heavy horse may at any moment drop from the sky on top of you.'

Daily Graphic

B— Hotel. Ideal home for married couples, temporary or permanent.

Advert in Liverpool paper

With the party is Mr H. Turner, reshipped to Rotterdam, where pulped preservative was added and attached to the delegation.

New Zealand paper

The steam trawler Ingoldsby, which had been undergoing overhaul in Grimsby graving-dock, sang mysteriously during Saturday night.

Edinburgh paper

What is more beautiful for a blonde to wear for formal dances than white tulle? My answer – and I'm sure you will agree with me – is 'Nothing'.

Worcester (Mass.) Evening Gazette

20-YEAR FRIENDSHIP ENDS
AT NASHVILLE ALTAR

Nashville paper

It has usually been the custom to get some prominent gentleman to take the chair, but on this occasion the selection fell on Councillor Eastland.

Bristol paper

He believed that with the assistance of the ladies it would be possible to form a non-profit-making concern.

Church magazine

Before going to sleep at night I read in bed for twenty minutes. During that time I warm my feet by breathing *in* through my nose and *out* through a length of rubber tubing reaching from my mouth to my feet. Within five minutes I am glowing with heat.

Letter in *Daily Mail* quoted in *New Statesman*'s 'This England' column

A man, operated on at a Darlington hospital, had in his stomach: hay, bits of metal and porcelain, a razor blade, a file, stones, a pin, 4½d., a football coupon, matches, a hair-grip, a key, nails, a pair of dividers, a pen-nib, a knife, and a double-six domino. He recovered.

Daily Express

'The boy would be expected to foresee,' Judge Forbes added, 'that there is one thing a man does not want after having his Sunday dinner; that is to have his feet tickled.'

News of the World

The wall simply had to go. So Pierre and his friends knocked it down. Then they smashed up a wooden partition. And at last they had carved a way out for the longest loaf in the world – all 24 ft and 116 lb of it.

Six men shouldered the monster loaf – baked for a bet – out of Pierre Bouchera's café in St Aygulf, in the South of France. Pierre did not mind the damage. He won his bet – and that was all that mattered.

Daily Mirror

Two or three years back, when at Watford, he dumped three in the net in 2 min. 52 sec. against Clapton Ointment.

Letter in Sunday paper

Sunrise tomorrow: 5.27 a.m.
High tide tomorrow: 8.57 a.m. and 9.25 p.m.
Checked by a policeman who had to use force.

Sussex paper

There was a baby in a perambulator near, and as the firework struck the ground it went off with a loud explosion.

Police Court News

Our directors and leaders look swell in their new sweaters, and in the near future it is hoped that they will be provided with a more complete uniform consisting of pants for the men and skirts for the young ladies.

Vancouver Sun

Please excuse John from school today as father's ill and the pig has to be fed.

Letter to schoolmaster

For sale. Quonset house in Douglas. Terms cash. All reasonable offers rejected.

Michigan paper

My children are good looking and healthy and appear to be normal but they are such little terrors that they are making my life unbearable. What is your advice? vice?

Waterbury (Connecticut) American

'I think we are stifling initiative here,' said Councillor H. Smithers, criticizing the action of the Highways Committee at the Widnes Town Council meeting on Tuesday night, in refusing an application from a local firm to pump waste acid over a public footpath.

Widnes Weekly News

A man in Perth, Australia, walked into a car dealer's showroom with a baby camel – and drove out in a new car. He was allowed £62 part-exchange for the three-month-old camel.

Weekend

A schoolmaster in Dundee told a court that he found this collection in a boy's pockets: two live wasps in an aspirin bottle; a gaspipe two-and-a-half feet long; the spiked top of an iron railing weighing 4 lbs; 30 ball bearings; four spark plugs; an unprotected razor blade; two ounces of home-made gunpowder; five yards of bandage and three heavy bolts.

When asked why he carried the gaspipe, the boy replied: 'I thought it might make an opium pipe like I have seen in pictures.'

In Madeira, a policeman searched the pockets of a seven-year-old boy who was suspected of theft. The policeman found six live worms, seven partly-smoked cigars, a dirty tape measure, a picture of a battle scene from World War II; 12 zip fasteners, a dagger – and a prayer book.

Weekend

My aunt has a mania for boiling things. On having trouble with her sewing-machine she put it in the boiler and boiled it. When the machine was taken out it worked as good as new.

Letter in *Woman's Own* quoted in *New Statesman*

FOR SALE – 9-column Burroughs adding machine. oGod condition. Apply Muskogee Shoe Store.

Oklahoma paper

The Rev. R. H. Maidstone made his first appearance in the pulpit at Palmerston Street Church, Castletown, on Sunday evening. The choir gave the anthem: 'Who is This, So Weak.'

Isle of Man Examiner

The service director said that the city had neither the money nor the equipment to restore the brides; they had deteriorated rapidly and were in need of extensive repairs.

Tiffin (Ohio) Tribune

Too often is a birthday made nothing more than an occasion for present giving and a party. It should have another side to it, if it is truly to be the subject for congratulations, small balls, flour and fry in boiling fat.

Hants paper

CHANNEL SWIM ATTEMPT

BOSTON GIRL'S ARRIVAL IN LIVERPOOL

Liverpool Echo

The best man was Mr William Hakesley, the gift of the bridegroom.

North London paper

While the main street at Bellingham was crowded with people, a van careered round the corner near the Fox and Hounds on two wheels at 50 m.p.h., causing a scrub mark 120 feet long. This was stated by Supt. J. Thompson at Bellingham magistrates' court on Wednesday when a 19-year-old man pleaded guilty to dangerous driving and also having a vehicle incapable of travelling either forward or backwards.

Northumberland paper quoted in *Daily Telegraph*

The Henley-on-Todd regatta took place at Alice Springs last Saturday. There was not a drop of water in the river. A crowd of 2,500 lined the banks of the Todd river to watch the crews running as they carried their bottomless yachts and skiffs over the sandy river bed. The head of the river for skiffs and the Australia cup for yachts were won by crews from Anoonguna aboriginal welfare settlement.

Australian News

Sir, – I have long been impressed by the omniscient commentaries on world-wide topics given by that individual described by the B.B.C. as 'Our Rhone Correspondent'.

Yours faithfully, Douglas Allen, 63 Hamilton Rd,
Thornton Heath.

The Times

Nearly 50 years ago Percy Holter gave his father his watch to look after while he was away fighting in World War I. His father lost it. Last week a workman found a watch in a drain at Pevensey Bay, Sussex. It was Percy's. And it still works.

The Sun

Sir Hugh and Lady C— received many congratulations after their horse's success. The latter wore a yellow frock trimmed with picot-edged frills and a close-fitting hat.

Berkshire paper

Gas range $15; washing machine $25; bird cage $4; baby cart $4; baby $15. Apply 519 E. 36th Ave.

Portland (Oregon) Shopping News

At the astonishment by missing a putt of not short fourth caused a gasp of quite eighteen inches.

Sporting paper

There will be many people, I fancy, who will welcome an opportunity to see this film a second time – if they were unfortunate enough to miss it on its first run.

Film Weekly

The bite of a mad dog is particularly dangerous if it is on the face or neck, the hands, or any other part of the body.

New Canaan (Connecticut) Advertiser

The last wicket fell just before lunchtime. After the interval a very pleasing improvement in the dimensions of the spectators was to be seen.

East Anglian Daily Times

George B— has had charge of the entertainment during the past year. His birth-provoking antics were always the life of the party and he will be greatly missed.

Willard (Ohio) Times

A *marriage in extremis* took place in Konsagaburg on the 6th inst., under the following circumstances. A widow named Kimbersber, aged 86, being on her death-bed, wished to bequeath the extensive brewery of which she was mistress, and all her other property, to a young man who was her foreman, and to whose long and faithful services she was chiefly indebted for her prosperity. Her lawyers informed her she could not defeat the claims of the collateral branches of the family, and upon this rendering she resolved to adopt the only mode left to her. She married the object of her goodwill, and died on the evening of the same day.

London paper quoted in *Curiosities of Matrimony*, 1889

A gentleman who paid some attention to a young lady near Portsmouth proposed marriage, which she declined on account of her youth (not a common reason). He begged her to name a time when he might expect a favourable answer. She replied in twenty years (her age being then 20). He paid strict attention to her, and at the expiration of that time reminded her of her promise, who, true to her word, accepted his hand, and they were married.

Curiosities of Matrimony, 1889

British Railways objected to a bus company running summer tours from West Hartlepool to Robin Hood's Bay, Yorkshire, because, an official said, there was an adequate train service.

But, the official told West Hartlepool's licensing authority, there would be no objection to the firm running a 'mystery tour'. What will be the 'mystery tour's' destination? Robin Hood's Bay, said the official, but the public won't know. The licence was granted.

Sunday Pictorial

'Why are you here today, Mr . . . . . Lomax?' Alice stumbled over the unfamiliar name. Mark reached out his hand to help her to her feet.

Woman's World

The bride, given away by her father, was being held in place by a wreath of orange blossoms.

Wedding report

It is unfortunately true of this age, as with every other age, that the poor can be defrauded with impunity, the Archbishop said.

See Banham Bros. List of used car bargains on page 9.

Hants paper

My daughter-in-law has the same name as that of law insists that she was taught by it belongs to this era even if it was his father, Madam. I hardly think her another to tell a widow, whose proper. Will you explain?

Letter in Manchester paper

She was a pathetic figure as she stood in the box, wearing a blue coat and a dark straw hat, with a spray of artificial trousers.

Liverpool paper

The success of the Conference has been in great measure due to the women shorthand writers who have been working all out in brief shifts.

New Zealand paper

DO NOT INTRODUCE
DOGS, STICKS, SUITCASES, TRESTLES, ETC,

Visitors are asked to deposit them in the cloakroom.

Sign outside Doge's Palace, Venice

In Oklahoma, 54-year-old Charlie Smith was driving steadily enough and at a moderate pace when police stopped him – because there was a horse sitting in the back seat of his car.

He explained: 'The poor old thing was looking so bored out there in the country I thought I'd bring him to town.' He was charged with being drunk while in control of a car and with stealing a horse.

Weekend

A man was making a phone call in Cannon Street underground station when it closed last night. The lights went out and he found all the exit gates locked.

He dialled 999. Said the operator: 'That's for life-and-death. Dial "O".' He dialed 'O' and spoke to the *same* operator, who told the City police.

News Chronicle

What I have said has demonstrated that it is very difficult to find an answer to that question, but if I were pressed for an answer I would say that, so far as we can see, taking it rather by and large, taking one time with another, and taking the average of Departments, it is probable that there would not be found to be very much in it either way.

Minutes of Evidence to Royal Commission on the Civil Service

The principal thing to remember when preparing a fork supper is to select only food which can be eaten comfortably on a plate with a fork. In the winter, hot bouillon or clear soup is always popular and can well be included.

Sunday paper

'This budget leakage is something that's got to stop,' said the President, with what seemed to be more than a trace of irrigation in his voice.

Jackson (Missouri) State Times

Mrs Ayling has let the muskrats use a room in her house as a workroom. This week they have made shell jewellery and painted Christmas boxes.

Waterbury (Connecticut) Republican

The bride was charmingly attired in white satin, and carried a bouquet of red carnations, and trailer.

Wedding report

LAMBING. A ewe, the property of Mr W. Tatham of Aberystwyth, has presented its owner with quadrupeds.

Welsh paper

NEW YORK CITY GOT AROUND TO ADOPTING A SAFETY SLOGAN TODAY. IT'S ZGREATEC XAFOY FOR ZGREATER NEW YORK.

U.S. News Despatch

A man I know locks up his alarm clock in a tin medicine chest (for extra noise) every night before retiring. To reach the key to open the chest to turn off the alarm he has to plunge his arm into a deep jug full of icy water where he dropped the key the night before. This is the only way he knows to be certain of waking up.

Sunday Graphic quoted in *New Statesman*'s 'This England'

Rochdale is to have a mobile barbecue at its centenary celebrations on Sept. 8. Because the site chosen for it in the town centre is in a smokeless zone, a whole ox will be roasted nearby on a trailer and towed over the border when the smoke has died down.

Daily Telegraph

The coroner (Mr W. Bentley Purchase) recorded an open verdict. He said: 'In many years of experience I have made the observation that if a woman is going to commit suicide she rarely takes her handbag.'

Evening Standard

I wish to take up lessons on the saxophone, but have high blood pressure, heart murmur, and punctured diaphragm. Do you think it would be advisable?

Health column in *The Graphic*

He said that he felt as Shadrach, Meschach or Abednego would have felt if, in the lion's den, they had been called on to propose the health and good appetite of the lions.

Warwickshire paper

Customers having left garments that are now over 30 days, are to be disposed of.

Cleaners' notice

MUST SELL. Plymouth 4-door Sedan,
complete with actress.
Call DE 4–3855.

Advert in *Philadelphia Enquirer*

Mrs Jenkins asserted that farm labourers did not get sufficient money to live properly, and therefore could not give of their best while sold for 2s. a dozen at Newport.

Welsh paper

The public house is a one-storey building and the occupants were sleeping upstairs.

Evening News

Bravo Porthcawl! It is something to be proud of to have the lowest infantile morality in the kingdom.

Welsh paper

The Powdra borzois have every opportunity of cultivating their brains, for Mrs Stilwell, having only a few, is able to give them the chance to become friendly and sensible.

Sporting paper

Everyone knows there is a good deal of difference between American newspapers and European ones. But what no one knew until the other day was that the American ones have a disastrous effect upon a certain bug. And the European ones leave the bug completely unimpaired. In fact, it's just possible that this discovery may be of enormous importance in insect pest control.

The story began when a Czech scientist, Dr Karel Slama, decided to visit the United States. He went to Harvard to carry on his work there for a time, and amongst his baggage was a batch of a certain insect he had been studying for many years. The insect was a hemipteran bug called Pyrrho-coris apterus. As soon as Dr Slama got to Harvard, he set about breeding this bug just as he had done back in Czechoslovakia. But though he did everything the same way, and the bugs were uninfluenced by the journey, their breeding behaviour in America was totally different. Like Peter Pan they never grew up. They entirely failed to transform into sexually mature adults at the end of the fifth larval stage. Some chemical was obviously acting as a hormone in preventing normal development. So, where was this chemical? What was keeping these Czech bugs permanently juvenile?

It so happened that a layer of paper towelling had been put on the floor of the insects' cages. And of course, this paper was American made rather than European. So the scientists at Harvard tested bugs with and without paper towelling in their cages. Sure enough, the bugs without paper developed normally. The scientists then tested twenty other brands of paper towelling. And eighteen of these twenty brands kept the insects immature.

To try and track this something to earth, Dr Slama and the Harvard scientists then tried all sorts of paper on the insects. They discovered that the *New York Times*, the *Wall Street Journal*, the *Boston Globe*, *Science*, and *Scientific American* all kept the insects immature. So they switched their attention over to paper from Europe, and found quite the opposite. *The Times* of London, for instance, and the scientific journal

Continued on p. 87

I make no promises to perform impossibilities as I have found in practice that these are very seldom carried out.

Election Candidate's letter

It is easy to slip on polished lino and the special flooring has been introduced in both saloons with this end in view.

Bournemouth paper

Household hint: Ink can more easily be removed from a white tablecloth before it is spilled than after.

Provincial paper

Shortly after 11 p.m. Stapylton ran across the road in answer to a call from Royal Infirmary suffering from head in a motor-car. She was taken to Oldham the other side and was knocked down by juries.

Manchester paper

The management reserves the right to remove any woman they consider proper.

Notice in dance hall

Another fur hint: if you want a fur to wear well, select one that will stand hard wear.

Fashion note

Alice paused, and, to hide her confusion, busied herself adjusting ornaments on the mantelpiece which need no adjusting. Then she turned her sweet flour-like face towards him.

Short Story

The bride also wore and carried a bouquet of Gloire-de-Dijon beige Court shoes and stockings to match.

Surrey paper

Nature, both highly mature papers, didn't keep their insects perpetually juvenile. And nor did any other European paper.

Plainly there was some crucial element in American paper. As yet this hasn't been discovered. But it surely will be, and then the scientists may have an excellent new method in their hands with which to combat insect pests. Also there's a good chance that this stuff will be a good deal less poisonous than most of the pesticides used today.

B.B.C. 'Science in Industry' programme

TAXMAN CRUSHED IN ORANGE JUICE CASE

Headline in *Evening Standard*

Do ham and iced tea taken at the same meal create a liquid in the stomach similar to ink? – Miss W.M.B.

I know of no scientific or dietetic reason why ham and iced tea taken at the same meal would create in the stomach a liquid similar to ink.

Good Housekeeping

CULTURED ex-lithographer, white, 45, with gold teeth, desires to get in touch with seven or eight musically inclined ladies in search of adventure.

Cupid's Columns, St Paul

The comfort in these buses is next to none.

Nigerian paper

The publishers promised to insert a slip in future editions acknowledging the sauce of passages quoted.

Berkshire paper

Time had rolled back a hundred years. People hurrying office-wards in the Strand waved their hats and raised a cheer to the immoral memory of Mr Pickwick.

Indian paper

In a costume of rosewood poiret twill, with hat to match, the happy pair left for their future home.

Canadian paper

One person was arrested last night on suspicion of being concerned in this morning's murders.

Jersey paper

They have acquired a pleasant country house in Berkshire for they are both lovers of the country, which they are having altered and decorated to their taste.

Theatrical paper

A twelve-year-old Birmingham boy who yesterday swallowed a needle was operated on today and removed from his stomach. He is going on as well as can be expected.

Provincial paper

Bedford firemen today received 28 letters thanking them for their efforts which destroyed 3 houses last Wednesday night.

Bedford paper

WANTED – Young or middle-aged woman who has small bald patch in her scalp wanted for demonstration of new hair insertion treatment. No compensation.

New York Times

Whereas, a lady, who called herself a native of Ireland, was in England in the year 1740, and resided some time at a certain village near Bath, where she was delivered of a son, whom she left, with a sum of money, under the care of a person in the same parish, and promised to fetch him at a certain age, but has not since been heard of: now this is to desire the lady, if living, and this should be so fortunate as to be seen by her, to send a letter directed to J.E., to be left at the Chapter Coffee-House, St Paul's Church-yard, London, wherein she is desired to give an account of herself and her reason for concealing this affair: or if the lady should be dead, and any person is privy to the affair, they are likewise desired to direct as above. N.B. this advertisement is published by the person himself, not from motives of necessity, nor to court any assistance (he being, by a series of happy circumstances, possessed of an easy and independent fortune), but with a real desire to know his origin. P.S. The strictest secrecy may be depended on.

Advert in *Falkner's Dublin Journal*

PERSONAL ITEMS

J. C. HAMLETT writes: 'My python, eleven and one-half feet long, weighing eighty-one pounds, died December one. I have not decided on next season at all, as I will have to have another big snake. For the winter I am again general foreman for the West Tennessee Fertilizer Company at Humboldt, Tenn.

The Billboard

The old aristocrat drove on without heeding the big bright tears of disappointment that rose to Peggy's lips.

Story in weekly paper

CHOICE WINES FOR SALE, being the property of a lady removed from a cellar in London.

Advert in weekly paper

Whenever eggs are cheap the fowls yield a fair supply, and when they become dear production stops.

Pall Mall Gazette

Alderman L—, J.P., the retiring Mayor, together with his lady, have filled the Mayoral chairs with dignity and decorum, rebounding with much credit to themselves and the Borough.

East Ham paper

This new loudspeaker is remarkable for its completely uniform rending of the musical scale.

Radio dealer's advert

Any experienced bridge player will realize that the message South has conveyed is this: 'I see probable game. It may be in Spades or in Hearts, or it may be in No Trumps, or perhaps in a minor suit.'

Sunday paper

AIREDALES – House-trained, safe with children, best protection against burglars or ladies living alone.

Advert in animal paper

BREAKS BOTH LEGS TURNING OVER IN BED

Headline in *The World*

Mrs Raymond Hackett and Miss Evelyn Fothergill gave a surprise pink and white shower for Mrs Mahlon Owens on the Eaton lawn, attended by 33 people. One feature of the programme was a Caesarian operation which proved amusing.

Vermont paper

LEAVE REGULATIONS – Section 3. When an employee absent from duty on account of illness dies without making application for advanced sick leave, the fact of death is sufficient to show a 'serious disability' and to dispense with the requirement of a formal application and a medical certificate.

U.S. Government order

Dear Sir,

I have the honour to resignate as my works are many and my salary are few. Besides which my supervising teacher makes many lovings to me to which I only reply, 'Oh, not, Oh, not.'

Letter from Phillipino woman teacher

The Evening of Clairvoyance on Tuesday
4th December at 7 p.m.,
has been cancelled owing to
unforeseen circumstances.

Notice in *East Kent Times*

The door opened and a girl came in – a slip of a girl with a firm little chin and a pair of lively grey ewes which gave Bernard a searching glance.

Australian paper

After this point the going was much easier and Bob called a halt. We lunched on some slabs of Kamet's red granite.

Travel book

The volumes consist of brief notes and fragments down at the moment of thought or observation on the back of an envelope, on the soles of his shoes while working in the street.

Review in literary weekly

Whatever your state of depression, remember always that it is only possible to stand erect as a Local Government Officer if you bend the knee effectively to the proper performance of work of social service.

Official magazine

One of the causes of unpleasantness was that the wife regarded her husband as being of a lower social order, his father having been an artesian.

New Zealand paper

SUET PUDDING. There are some people who cannot make a suet pudding successfully. These are better steamed.

Lancashire paper

Local craftsmen in Nigeria buy empty Milk of Magnesia bottles for a penny each and melt them into blue beads. Then they string them together and sell 400 a week to tourists at 3s. 6d. a time. The Milk of Magnesia public relations department is sending out strings of these beads, accompanied by a hand-out which says 'the reason Nigerians seem to consume so much Milk of Magnesia is evident by the extremely constipated and indigestible type of diet they eat.'

Sunday Times

Sir, – In connection with your interesting letter of last Sunday, a French lady of my acquaintance went into a high-class confectionery shop here and, pointing to a certain kind of cake, said: 'I would like one of those cakes, please.'

The assistant eyed her with a little contempt and said, 'Those aren't cakes; they're gâteaux.'

W. G. Scholes, Leeds.

The Guardian

'Nothing annoys me more than finding a few stray maggots under the grill when I am about to do the toast for breakfast,' says Mrs V. M. Hart of West Drayton, whose husband is a keen angler.

Mr Hart, according to his wife, likes to keep a tin of gentles handy in the refrigerator. This, she says, is bad enough, but sometimes when the cold has made them lethargic, he warms them up under the grill.

Daily Telegraph

Gainsborough Rural Council on Tuesday decided that the nudist camp of the East Midlands Sunfolk Society of Nottingham is a playing field for the purpose of Section 8 of the Rating and Valuation Act and qualifies for rate relief.

Lincolnshire Chronicle

None but a novice in economics would expect Denmark, or any other country, to buy from us exactly as much as we sell to her.

Weekly paper

UNDERTAKER'S FAILURE

– – –

LET DOWN BY CUSTOMERS

Headlines in Yorks paper

At a street corner in Los Angeles the flood washed out electric light poles and live wives fell spluttering into the street.

New Zealand paper

Miss Hazel Foster's gladioli garden has been attracting considerable attention of late. She spends many hours among her large collection of pants.

Pennsylvania paper

Bishop K— has once again in the role of censor of the modern young woman's dress. He has laid it down definitely that no dress should be worn above the knees.

New Zealand paper

JACK'S LAUNDRY

Leave your clothes here, ladies, and spend the afternoon having a good time.

Advert in New Mexico paper

WANTED – unlimited quantity of fig leaves. Tel: Brighton 0000 after 7 p.m.

Advert in *Brighton Evening Argus*

At 27, Clodagh is married to company director Desmond O'Kennedy and his three boys under five and a seven-bedroomed Georgian house set in an acre of garden.

South London Press

HOW THE BULGARIAN AMBASSADOR UPSET MRS HUNT'S HOT DOGS

Headline in *Daily Mail*

London Transport's bus cleaners have to fill in a form if they have experienced an 'irregularity or occurrence'. I quote from a West Indian bus cleaner:

'As I was cleaning from the top floor all my tickets and rubbish, my box is at the top, my feet catch the box and I nok it down and I fell down with it. When the bottom cum, my box noks down my buket.

I go up from the bottom and my brush is at the top and I step on it and I slip and I throw my box to the bottom.

I go down to fetch my box and I step on it and slip again as my other foot goes into the buket which has the water and I fall again with my foot in the buket.

I come out of the buket and I fill it with water I put it on the top stairs and I go down to my box to bring it up and at the top I step over my buket with my foot but it is wet from being in the buket and I fall back down the stairs and I am hurt.

I am going to put water in my buket again wen Mr Chandler say why I am cleaning *his* bus and I hit him with my buket and I am sorry.'

Henry Fielding column, *The Sun*

The cost of nude models has shocked the rate-payers of a seaside town. More models are needed by the art college at Bournemouth. And that means an extra £800 on the yearly £2,200 bill for models' fees.

Town Councillor, Harold Heath, who is a chairman of Bournemouth's Federation of Ratepayers, said last night: '£800 is a lot of money . . . I think expenditure of this sort should be cut to the bare minimum.'

Daily Mirror

'Get on with it!' shouted the crowd, as half-back James paused with his foot on the ball. He did, and it produced a goat.

Sports news in Sunday paper

Michael M—, who toured with the All Blacks, at the match on Saturday last kicked three gals in succession.

New Zealand paper

The item £1,631 for Centenary Entertainment will not occur again in the near future.

Report of a learned society

The kick-off is at 3.15, and the teams will be found elsewhere.

Cambridge Daily News

You will be glad to hear that your former Rector, Archdeacon B—, has had both of his operations for the sinus trouble, and is now fooling very well indeed. He had no difficulty in taking all his Christmas services.

Church magazine

For Sale – 3 actual real photographs: Mussolini, 3 stages death: on ground, hanging with two others, one a woman, and in coffin, macabre: offers. Box XZ 1943.

Exchange & Mart

A MAN DROWNED BY A CRAB

June 30, 1811. A few days ago, John Hall, a labouring man, went at low water among the rocks at Hume Head for the purpose of catching crabs, when meeting with one in the interstices of the rocks, of a large size, he imprudently put in his hand, for the purpose of pulling it out; the animal, however, caught his hand between its claws or forceps, and, strange as it may appear, kept its hold so firmly, that every effort on the part of the poor fellow to extricate himself proved ineffectual; and no one being at hand to assist him, the tide came in and he was next morning found drowned.

Kirby's Wonderful & Eccentric Museum, 1820

Old-established manufacturer of suspension bridges requires door-to-door salesman.

African paper

(Here and in the item below we see Gobfrey Shrdlu at his best. He is perhaps trying to tell us that the life we lead is too humdrum. We should have imagination. . . .)

Man doing heavy work requires old sports jackets, 38 in., cheap, also dozen babies napkins, 24 in., good condition.

Exchange & Mart

FOR SALE – Granite-faced Gentleman's residence in St Saviour's.

Advert in Jersey paper

The outbuildings include a heated greenhouse and petting shed.

Estate Agents' list

Resisting the temptation to shoot himself at close range, he cleverly flicked the ball sideways to Humphries.

The Times

Pedigree Scotch Terriers For Sale.
Dog and Bitch Puppies, by sons of
Ch. Malgen Juggernaut; dam well bred.

Advert in *Cumberland Herald*

When will people living in Station Cottages be rehoused because if these houses are not soon demolished they will fall down. Rain comes down the walls like water.

Nottingham Evening Post

If two and two are put together the cat comes out of the bag.

Indian paper

INVISIBLE MENDING. British Officer says: 'I was astonished when I got back the job I gave you – it didn't look like a darned suit at all!'

From a circular

The Rev. Mr Hagemore, who lived at Calthorn in Leicestershire, kept one servant of each sex, whom he locked up every night. His last employment in the evening was to go round his premises, let loose his dogs, and fire his gun. Going on the morning of the 1st January, 1746, as usual to release his servants one of his dogs suddenly fawned upon him, and threw him into a pond, where the water was breast high. His servants heard him call for assistance, but being unable to quit their prisons, he was drowned.

At the time of his death he had thirty gowns and cassocks, fifty-eight dogs, one hundred pair of breeches, one hundred pair of boots, four hundred pair of shoes, eighty wigs, though he always wore his own hair, eighty wagons and carts, eight ploughs, and used none, fifty saddles, and furniture for the menage, thirty wheelbarrows, and so many walking-sticks that a toy-man in Leicester Fields offered eight pounds for them. He had about sixty horses and mares, three hundred pick-axes, two hundred spades and shovels, twenty-five ladders, and two hundred and forty razors.

Kirby's Wonderful & Eccentric Museum

WANTED – Single Room with bath for music lesson, vicinity Galle face.

Advert in *Times of Ceylon*

WOMAN LEAPS FROM COFFIN, IS KILLED

MOINESTI, Rumania, Wednesday. Mourners of the burial of Anna Bochinsky were astonished to see the 'dead' woman jump out of her coffin while it was being carried with the lid open – as is the custom in Rumania – from the cemetery to the grave.

She ran into the road and was run over and killed by a motor-car.

Daily Express

WE EXCHANGE EVERYTHING –
BICYCLES, WASHING MACHINES, ETC., ETC.
Bring Your Wife and get the
deal of your life

Sign in shop window

Large quantities of herring and sprats have been netted by the Avock fishermen in the Inverness Town Hall during the past week.

Highland Leader

Foreman wanted, to take charge of females, sandpapering turned legs.

Advert in *Bury Free Press*

The size of the crowd could not be estimated for three-quarters of it was invisible.

Liverpool paper

Mrs N—, who won a leg of mutton, kindly gave her prize bark and this raised 10s. for the funds.

Dorset paper

IN THIS HALL ON SUNDAY 6 p.m.
THE DEVIL

Notice outside North London Hall

WANTED, companion for two ladies in bath (Som.)

The Lady

TROUSER SEATS BEAR THE BRUNT OF WEAR

Qualitatively it may be evident that the seats of trousers wear out faster than other parts. Quantitative information on the point – obtained in a study of the wearing qualities of serge – is now available. (*Textile Research Journal*, Vol. 35, p. 1035.) The trousers studied, tailored to a cadet-uniform specification from serge woven from a medium-quality wool, were worn by volunteer senior students at an American university.

Each of the students was supplied with two pairs of the trousers, to be worn in alternate weeks. . . . The trousers were visually examined at intervals; quantitative data on the degrees of wear at various points were obtained when the service life was considered to be over. . . . On the basis of their fitness for wear at college, the service lives of the trousers ranged from 1,323 to 2,926 hours, varying of course with the build, activity, and carefulness of the wearers. Wear of the serge was apparent from thin or threadbare areas, such as the knees and thighs. Bursting tests showed that the wear of these points was about equal, loss of strength of the failure at these locations being respectively 37 and 39 per cent. The greatest wear was, however, at the seat, where the fabric had lost 62 per cent of its original strength.

A rather mystifying narrow curved stretch of abrasion low in the seat of a few of the trousers ultimately was found to be due to the habit of some of the students of striking matches there.

New Scientist

ADVERTISER invites any person interested in the science of physics to disprove that the product of the numerical values of the velocity of light and Newton's constant of gravitation are equal to the integral number, two thousand; no prize. – Write Box D 1924, *The Times*, E.C.4.

The Times

Spring cabbage plants 2s 6d. per 9 ft, fitted with electric.

Advert in *Market Drayton Advertiser*

The engagement is announced between John Christian, eldest son of Mr and Mrs Andreas, and Violent Jean, elder daughter of Mr and Mrs Benson, Kinrosshire.

Ramsey Courier

The lake at Danson Park has been remarkably immune from drowning accidents. There have been a number of fatalities but very few accidents.

Local paper

Gaudy cottons for garden and country are striped like a zebra in scarlet, blue, green, yellow, and purple.

Daily Sketch

'Today', she said, and he held up his thumb and grinned at her. If only this could be for ever, the two of them alone. But the sea lifted the boat like a sullen cork, and he stopped thinking about anything but handling her.

John Bull

Whether shooting his best friend at sea, or in bed with his employer's wife, Ferguson remains the same bowler-hatted and inhibited Englishman.

Book review in *The Observer*

'I got something off my chest today that's been hanging over my head for some time. That's behind me now, thank goodness.'

Film star on B.B.C. interview

NORWICH, June 24., From our correspondent:

As the ward staff would give little information, a patient in the Norfolk and Norwich Hospital hit on a novel way to check on his progress towards recovery. He asked for the bedside telephone provided by Friends of Hospitals, and, after dialling the hospital, asked to be put through to the ward he was in.

He asked the ward sister: 'How is Mr So-and-So today? How did his operation go, and are there any complications?' After more questions the ward sister asked: 'Are you a relative?' 'No', came the reply, 'I am Mr So-and-So.'

Mr Francis Pointer, vice-chairman of the Friends of Hospitals, said afterwards: 'The story is perfectly true, but we are not revealing the name of the man.'

The Times (by permission)

Receptionist-telephonist required . . . must be prepared to work an occasional Saturday morning (quite often)·'

Advert in *Manchester Evening News*

A friend who was at London Airport yesterday reports that a schoolboy in the Oceanic Building was carrying a suitcase labelled: 'Passenger to Hongkong (via Tulse Hill).'

Evening Standard

OSCAR FARTHINGALE, of 33 Aylmer Drive, Teddington, Surrey, wishes it to be known that this is not an assumed name, but is the one recorded on his birth certificate.

Personal Column, *The Times*

Who composed the celebrated *Dream of Gerontius*? – Beethoven, Elgar, Mozart, Weber, or Wagner? or an abdominal muscle?

Quiz feature in Glasgow paper

THE WAY TO HIS HEART might lie in the tricky art of cooking his liver.

She, cookery supplement

The radio said that Russia's sole condition was that such talks should not be made dependent on any condition.

Daily Express

When the motion was carried, the Mayor presented a gold medallion to the Retiring Mayor, and the Mayoress to the Retiring Mayoress.

Oldham Evening Chronicle

An Arab country, like Ireland, is a place where the remarkable seldom happens, and the impossible is of frequent occurrence.

Daily Telegraph

The Royal yacht steamed up the river between steamers gaily decorated, and later drove in an open carriage through densely crowded streets lined by six battalions of infantry.

Glasgow paper

Mrs J. Gearing of Sebring, Florida, is visiting this week in the home of Mrs Melvina Burtis. Mrs Gearing died a few years ago.

Ludlow (*Vermont*) *Tribune*

A California motorist who passed a red stop signal told police: 'If I make any sudden moves my wife spills her breakfast and that makes her mad.'

Sure enough, inside the car, the wife was tucking into a plateful of bacon and eggs.

Daily Express

MANY COOKS IN
UNEXCITING
'SWAN LAKE'

Headline in *Daily Mail*

Alenčina dobrodružství v podzemní říši
Alicia en Terra de Meravelles
Alice i Vidunderland
Alice's avonturen in het wonderland
Elsje's avonturen in 't wonderland
Aventures d'Alice au pays des merveilles
Alice's Abenteuer im Wunderland
Alisz Kalandjai Csodaországban
Le Avventure d'Alice nel paese delle meraviglie
Else i eventyrland efter Lewis Carroll
Ala w Krainie czarow
Прикпюченія Алисы В'ъ странѣчудес'ъ
Elisi katika nchi ya ajabu
Alices märkvärdiga äventyr i underlandet
Anturiaethau Alys yng Ngwlad Hud

British Museum General Catalogue

AUTHORITIES in Peking, China, are campaigning to stop Chinese women from knitting in public buses. In recent months several passengers have been treated for knitting-needle wounds received when buses have stopped suddenly. 'It is our earnest expectation that all women will not jeopardize the safety of others on the bus,' said one official.

Weekend

Is it from irregular meals or from an unhealthy home? Or is your weak state hereditary? Has it come down to you through your parents? In any case remove the cause.

From a popular medical book

NOTICE
No cars or cycling
on these footpaths
is prohibited

Notice in Berwick-on-Tweed

Two private inquiry agents said they had climbed 20 ft up a popular tree near King's Lynn Flats, Ithaca Road, to watch a bedroom in Mrs C—'s flat one night.

The Sun, Sydney

Busts, which ceased to matter last season, seem to have disappeared altogether, except for evening when they pop rather startlingly above the neck line.

Evening Standard

Their impression of Gordon's distillery? Cleanliness and efficiency were the two things that particularly impressed them, they told me. They were also very taken with the obvious happiness of the employees.

Morning Advertiser

If the patient faints when standing up he collapses on to the ground.

First-Aid Manual

Anton Morvet's donkey liked cream puffs so much he broke a cake shop window and scoffed every cake in sight. The donkey was ill for three days, but it cost Anton £11 to pay for the damage to the shop.

The Sun

About forty years ago, at one of the provincial Assizes, a gentleman was tried and convicted, upon circumstantial evidence of the murder of his niece. The circumstances sworn to were as follows: That the uncle and the niece were seen walking in the fields; that a person at a small distance heard the niece exclaim – 'Don't kill me, Uncle! Don't kill me!' – and that instant a pistol or fowling-piece was fired off. Upon these circumstances the gentleman was convicted and executed. Near twelve months after, the niece, who had eloped, arrived in England, and hearing of the affair, elucidated the whole transaction. It appeared that she had formed an attachment for a person whom her uncle disapproved: when walking in the fields, he was earnestly dissuading her from the connexion, when she replied that she was resolved to have him, or it would be her death, and therefore said, 'Don't kill me, Uncle! Don't kill me!'

At the moment she uttered these words a fowling-piece was discharged by a sportsman in a neighbouring field. The same night she eloped from her uncle's house, and the combination of these suspicious circumstances, occasioned his ignominious death.

Kirby's Wonderful & Eccentric Museum, 1820

In last week's notebook under the heading 'What's in a name', the name of a Honolulu councillor was misspelt as Mr Kekoalaulionapalihauliulio David Kaapuawaokamehaheha.

This should have read: Mr Kekoalauliionapalihauliulio David Kaapuawaokamehaheha.

Municipal Journal

Prods with the office ruler only provoked more violent movement, and at last one officer cut open the bag with his sabre, and two boa-constrictors quickly left the room and slammed the door.

Exeter Express

Even today it is possible to be fitted so perfectly that a woman can lift herself up out of her corset, move her body around, and drop back into it, without moving the corset in the slightest.

Boston Teachers' News Letter

LADY NURSE. Experienced infant preferred. Entire charge.

Advert in *The Lady*

An opportunity will shortly be available for a secretary of impeachable character, in a small office, of a new industry shortly opening near Redruth.

West Briton

Gentleman has several small houses let to tenants he wishes to dispose of.

Dalton's Weekly

♊ ♌ SAGGITARIUS (Nov 22–Dec 22). Precautions ♐ ♋
♈ ♒ should be taken against running into unforeseen ♍ ♉
♎ ♏ occurrences or events. ♑ ♓

News Chronicle

A RAT, lately visiting a tub of oysters at the post office in Falmouth, and whisking his tail between the open shells of one of them, it closed upon him, and held him so firmly that he was prevented from escaping through his hole, and was found in the morning with the oyster still holding fast of his tail at the entrance of it.

La Belle Assemblée, 1800

A wooden leg has been hung up in the bar of the Fox and Hounds at Singleton, in Sussex. It turned up in a local cowshed and someone remembered that the village carpenter had made it for a three-legged bull 40 years ago.

The Sun

AN ENGLISH PUB IN NEW YORK'S GREENWICH VILLAGE

an authentic pub serving genuine English scones

The Village Voice quoted in *The Sun*

Sir, – I would not presume to object to the Road Research Board's playing statistical games with their fragments of information (your report on July 27), but it would be well for them to realize that such a phrase as 'of the remaining 80 per cent, 24 per cent (28 drivers)' is less precise, scientific, and meaningful than '28 of the 141 drivers'.

It is probably only a matter of time before a mathematically minded bishop informs us that of the disciples chosen by Jesus no fewer than 8·3 per cent betrayed Him.

Yours faithfully, H. L. EVANS,
Lecturer in Religious Education, Bangor

The Times

LONDON MARKED PLATES required, complete set. Exchange grandfather, or cash.

Exchange & Mart

Britain's latest and most up-to-date atom power station has as its centre-piece a unique giant steel sphere 135 feet in diameter, constructed to house a fast-breeding rector.

Cyprus Mail

LARGE SECRETARY With Swelled Front Excellent Condition $50

Advert in *Van Huys News*, California

In 'The Night is Departing' chorus, a base lead was missed, partly because one of the singers was, I noticed, so deaf that he could not see the conductor.

Berkshire paper

Miss Kailer tossed her head seeking the first robin and lilted the gay and carefree song in an easy childlike manner. One felt the shivering anticipation of a young girl running up the spine.

Harrisburg (Virginia) Daily News-Record

Practise the art of deep breathing. After the morning bath take a deep breath, retain it as long as possible, then slowly expire.

Home Chat

The Bishop remained motionless, but a woman rushed wildly to the front of the platform and endeavoured to agree with the Vicar, whom she hit on the back with an umbrella.

Suffolk paper

U.S. Air Force General Don Flickinger said last night that all chimpanzees used in space flights would be volunteers. He was asked how chimpanzees could volunteer. He replied: 'We hold an apple in one hand and a banana in the other. If they choose the banana, they are judged to have volunteered. They almost always choose the banana.'

Daily Express

Till now, the most formidable obstacle in the path of a man wishing to use his own telephone has been a woman. But other hazards have lately come over the horizon. An unfortunate gentleman in Bridlington, Yorkshire, has for the past two years been receiving calls from America, Germany, Switzerland and all over the world, asking him if he is 'the ambassador'. These diplomatic inquiries come in a wide variety of languages and at all hours of the day and night. The recipient does his best in the Yorkshire language to get over the point that he is not anybody's ambassador and is doubtless grateful that, thus far, no one has declared war on him. The telephone men explain that the overseas calls keep coming because foreign operators keep dialling the wrong code for some unknown embassy and, since such human errors are remotely uncontrollable, nothing can be done unless the Bridlington gentleman changes his number.

New Scientist

WANTED, man to work on rubbish, junk and garbage truck. Must be college graduate with high IQ.

Massachusetts paper quoted in *The Sun*

Manuel Walters of the Malay Mob awoke in a temper. His anger was caused by the six ·22 bullets which had thudded into him as he slept.

Drum

Slowly, almost one by one, Ordway's eyes followed the new steps in the snow.

from '*The White Tower*'

A large row of pink earls belonging to a well-known lady of noble birth has been restored to her.

South Wales Echo

Communicate direct to Transport Officer in case of accidents. As members give their services voluntarily, reasonable notice should be given – 24 hours whenever possible.

Gloucester paper

Four grown-ups and four children made up the tight bridesmaids who arrived with the best man.

Coventry paper

GRAPEFRUIT LATE TELLING POLICE OF INJURED MAN

Headline in Pennsylvania paper

(To my mind this item illustrates vividly the genius of Gobfrey Shrdlu. Instantly he has us speculating – what grapefruit, and why, oh why was it late in telling the police? We become so hypnotized by our train of thought that we cannot bear to read the item below the headline in case the explanation is prosaic – D.P.)

A conference of the Ministers of departments concerned will take place in London to arrange measures for their execution.

Essex paper

There is certainly a world of difference between maternity observed and maternity from within. I had not realized, for example, that one got bigger not only in front but also in the flank and round the face: 'Your trouble,' my husband said, 'is that you don't understand the principles of aircraft construction. How can you expect to add extra passenger space without increasing the fuel storage and wingspread?'

Katharine Whitehorn in *The Observer*

RAM-ROD IN HEAD

Many eminent doctors are reminded of a marvellous surgical case by the news of the death of Arthur Doades, an inmate of the Spalding Infirmary. In July, 1898, when 15, Doades was scaring birds for a farmer, and while ramming down powder, the gun went off.

The ram-rod entered Doades's forehead and passed out of the top of his head, carrying the boy's cap with it. Cap and ram-rod were found together some distance off. Although his life was at first despaired of, Doades eventually recovered. The case excited such interest that leading doctors from London and elsewhere investigated it before they would be convinced that such a thing was possible.

News of the World, 1926

Sir, – Mr Ascoli's metric version of 'Full fathom five' recalls the version of a student at a training college for teachers who was instructed to make a paraphrase of that song. His rendering was as idiotic as the setting of the exercise: 'Your male parent's body is deposited at a depth of thirty feet.'

I am, Sir, your obedient servant,
R. M. Inge, Ipswich, Suffolk
The Times

Dear Madam,
In reply to your letter, we are very sorry for the delay in sending the House-coat, but the tremendous demand for these has denuded our stock. We are, however, expecting further delay now in a day or so.

Yours obediently,
Blank Bros Ltd.

NEW MILTON, Hants. – Between sea and New Forest. Comfortably furnished detached MOUSE to LET.

Church Times

A Handley Page, with two Rolls-Royce engines, was the first and only machine to fly to India, and was the first and only machine to fly to India, and is the second to fly to India.

Norfolk paper

I have been very bilious all night and it has left me with a very bad head. I hope to shake it off today.

Letter to an employer

The only lot of any consequence was a drawing by Degas of Carlo Pellegrini smoking a cigarette (23 in. by 12½ in.) which fetched £96.

Weekly journal

Mr William Duncan of North Dakota stopped here on his way to Fostoria to say hell to his many friends today.

Medina (Ohio) Sentinel

Der jammerwoch

Es brillig war. Die schlichte Toven
  Wirrten und wimmelten in Waben;
Und aller-mümsige Burggoven
  Die mohmen Räth' ausgraben.

Bewahre doch vor Jammerwoch!
  Die Zähne knirschen, Krallen kratzen!
Bewahr' vor Jubjub-Vogel, vor
  Frumiösen Banderschnätzchen!

Er griff sein vorpals Schwertchen zu,
  Er suchte lang das manchsam' Ding;
Dann, stehend unten Tumtum Baum,
  Er an-zu-denken-fing.

Als stand er tief in Andacht auf,
  Des Jammerwochen's Augen-feuer
Durch tulgen Wald mit wiffeln kam
  Ein burbelnd Ungeheuer

Eins, zwei! Eins, zwei! Und durch und durch
  Sein vorpals Schwert zerschnifer-schnück,
Da blieb es todt! Er, kopf in Hand,
  Geläumfig zog züruck.

Und schlugst Du ja den Jammerwoch?
  Umarme mich, mein Böhm'sches Kind!
O Freuden-Tag! O Halloo-Schlag!
  Er chortelt froh-gesinnt.

Es brillig war, &c.

Macmillan's Magazine, Feb. 1872

(This version of Jabberwocky appears in a letter signed 'Thomas Chatterton', and has been attributed to Dr Robert Scott, then Dean of Rochester.)

A Wisconsin woman told the court in seeking a divorce that the retired naval officer she married insisted that they sleep in a hammock. In 23 years of marriage she had fallen out 16 times and felt she was getting too old for such insecurity. Decree granted.

London Opinion

To let, Furnished Service House; 2 reception and 5 bedrooms; no servant worries, we provide them.

Advert in West London paper

The audience included the Duchess of R— and Lady C—, who motored over from Salisbury and embraced a large number of lovers of music in the district.

Wiltshire paper

An almost incredible fightffl, if it can be called a fightffl, took place in the very harbour of Kronstadt itself.

Scotch paper

North Side, nice 4-bedroomed home, possession 15 days. Colonel B— lived in this place 2 years and is in very good condition.

San Antonio News

Sir, – I have read with interest the letters on ramblers' attire. For men, I do not think there is anything more serviceable than shorts. I am a female rambler, but I find a tweed shirt and pullover enough. Yours, etc.

Letter in Lancs paper

I do hope that Accrington Town Council will lay these precepts to their hearts, which in Latin I will quote: 'Quod Hoc Sibi Vult.' It means that exposed foodstuffs will not only be impregnated with volcanic-like dust from the town's horrible organic refuse, but will also be tainted with the smell that tastes.

Accrington Gazette

A firm of cracker manufacturers at Norwich are trying to contact a sailor to return an engagement ring and 10s. he sent them in 1927. He wanted the firm to put the ring in a cracker and send it to his girl friend. But he gave no address, so the gift was never sent.

The Sun

As the huge jetliner screeched to an emergency stop half-way down the runway, fire tenders and engineers raced out to meet it. But there was no need for panic. The Boeing 707 landing at Anchorage Airport, Alaska, had just been charged by a drunken moose. It was slightly dented.

The moose, probably with a bit of an ache in its antlers, lurched back into the bush for a long sleep.

Weekend

Eight new houses, not yet occupied, were broken into on Saturday at a building estate off Chelsfield-lane, where locks and window catches were damaged.

'We thought at first it was vandals at work,' said the site foreman, Mr W. Bennett. Then it was found that the only thing stolen was a primrose-coloured lavatory pan. In one of the houses a similar coloured pan was broken, while the remaining six all had bathroom fittings of a different shade,

'We had a pedestal basin in the same primrose shade stolen from the site before Christmas; so we think the thief came back and went through the houses till he found the type he wanted,' added Mr Bennett. 'He must have damaged one trying to get it out and went on to find another.'

Kentish Times

An ostrich that turns a blind eye to other aspects of the hobby will inevitably become a boomerang.

A handyman's magazine

Once you have dealt with us you will recommend others.

Advert in *East Kent Mercury*

My reference to gargoyles – and I am still without any explanation of the ones anciently in Eastgate – reminds me that I recently had a lady from the Norton area call to see me.

Gloucester Citizen

In view of the typhoid epidemic, hotel guests are assured that all vegetables have been boiled in water specially passed by the manager.

Notice in Cyprus hotel

Good Home offered elderly lady in return for assisting young mother with refined week-old baby.

Advert in New Zealand paper

FOR SALE – A large stone gentleman's diamond ring, set in a solid gold band.

Advert in *Cork Examiner*

The *Saturday Evening Post* recently enlightened its readers with a little item about a fox in southern Illinois that got rid of its fleas by backing into a pond while holding a tuft of wool in its mouth. The fleas 'had hastily crawled up through his fur and taken refuge in the wool' which the cunning fox released once he was completely submerged, thus ridding himself of his 'tiny tormenters'.

Those who are unable to procure a back number of the *Post* will find the same story in John Swan's *Speculum Mundi*, 1643. He says he got it from the *Historia* of Olaus Magnus, 1555. Olaus doesn't say where he got it.

from *The Natural History of Nonsense* by Bergen Evans

A man in Denver, Colorado, was arrested after stealing some sparking plugs from the factory where he worked. When police searched his home they found it stacked with 290,000 plugs.

He said: 'I just like to see them around.'

Weekend

In the year 1796, died at Wardley Workhouse, Berks, Mary Pitts, aged 70; on being accused of having rummaged the box of another pauper, she wished God might strike her dead if she had; and instantly expired.

Kirby's Wonderful & Eccentric Museum

Sir, – The problem of shoes has many aspects and one solution may be provided by a lady who purchased a very expensive pair. After wearing them three times they were worn out and fell to pieces. On voicing her complaint to an assistant in the shop, she was told, more in sorrow than in anger: 'I am sorry, madam, we do not cater for pedestrians.'

W. FAIRCLOUGH, Principal, Kingston College of Art.

The Times

Before passing, however, attention should be drawn to a remarkable collection of local beetles – modestly encased in drawers, but really one of the wonders of the exhibition.

Aberdeen paper

Dr S— is associated with societies for the prohibition of cruel sports, recorder playing and Welsh folk songs.

Yorkshire Post

FOAM CUSHIONS – As an introduction into the rubber trade we offer foam rubber cushions at rock bottom prices.

Advert in *Ayrshire Post*

This week's hint. When speaking or singing be sure to turn your face to the audience as far as possible. One hundred and twenty first quality eggs should weigh 17 lbs.

From a theatre programme

In 1911 he worried Mrs Laura Little of Montgomery, Alabama. They have three children.

Philadelphia Inquirer

A new insect bomb said to be non-poisonous to humans but stronger than DDT in its effect comes in a 16-ounce pressurized can tagged $1.89 in Horn's Housewares department. Ask for Safelex.

Whether you eat 'em as breakfast rolls or with supper you'll keep on eating till the box is empty! Oh my, but they do taste good.

Pittsburgh Post-Gazette

Motor vehicle safety belts must be installed rigidly enough to withstand a sudden thirst.

Trenton Times

HALL *v.* HYDER

The LORD CHIEF JUSTICE said that the facts as found by the justices were merely that there had been consumption in the bar of licensed premises by a person under the age of 18 of shandy, being a mixture of beer and lemonade, and that the respondent was the holder of a license in respect of the premises.

In the present case, the justices had come to the conclusion that shandy was not intoxicating liquor within the Act of 1964 in that it had not been shown by the prosecution that the liquor was of a strength exceeding two degrees of proof.

In his Lordship's judgement, the justices had come to the wrong conclusion, and he based his judgement on a very short ground. It was clear that what the respondent had sold, and all that he could sell, was beer and, quite separately, lemonade. His Lordship said 'all that he could sell' because again, if one went back to the Act of 1952, one found that by section 163(1), he could not sell beer diluted with any other substance: 'If any dealer in or retailer of beer dilutes any beer or adds anything to beer other than finings for the purpose of clarification he shall be liable to a penalty of fifty pounds . . .' That had been held to forbid the mixing of a weaker and inferior beer with a stronger beer, and, as shown by Crofts *v.* Taylor (1887) 19 Q.B.D. 524, it did not prevent the publican from selling 'half and half', provided that that was done in the customer's presence and as his agent. In other words, what the publican did when he sold shandy was to sell beer, and lemonade or ginger beer, and then, as the consumer's agent, to pour one into the other.

Starting there, if what was sold was beer, it was perfectly apt to say that that beer was consumed albeit it was later mixed with some other ingredient.

True it could be said that, when the mixing took place, a new liquor was formed, but beer was sold, for consumption on the premises, and it was allowed to be consumed on the premises, notwithstanding that it was mixed with lemonade.

Law report in *The Times* (by permission)

Chestnut fencing and
garden screening.
Illustrated cat on
request.

Gardening weekly

WANTED – Gardener; must be experienced, or useless.

Advert in Wilts paper

Catherine had always been lucky. Even the sun was shining when she first saw it.

Everybody's

If Mr Marjoribanks had touched on this question it would have sharpened his axe; by doing so he would have caught more fish later on.

South London paper

Lady in Black Velvet Dinner Gown (38 bust, 5 ft 8 in. figure), £5

Advert in *The Lady*

Wieboldt's New Gourmet Shop . . . for the amateur chef . . . for the epicure, or for the *coup de grace* of any meal or party.

Advert in Glencoe (Illinois) paper

Our picture shows the Berlin Bowling Club team which won the Ladies' Fencing Contest for Austria.

Caption in illustrated paper

POSITION WANTED

CATALOGUER, male, middle-aged, malicious, misanthropic, unprepossessing in manner and appearance, fed to teeth with supervisor's woes, wants exorbitant salary for cataloguing job demanding few contacts with colleagues and patrons. 17 years special and university library experience. Large Ontario city preferred. Address replies to Room 894, 63 Perkin St, Ottawa, Ontario.

Canadian librarians' journal

Walter Rutter, from Rugely, Staffordshire, was working at the coal face in Lea Hall Colliery when his upper and lower sets of teeth fell out. He thought he would never see them again.

The teeth were carried 1,400 yards along conveyor belts, then 100 yards up a shaft with tons of coal. Half a mile later, travelling in a tub on another belt, they were dumped into a 150-ton bunker which was being sprayed by powerful hoses.

Afterwards the errant dentures were loaded into a railway truck with a consignment of coal. The upper half turned up in a housewife's coal shed. She returned them to the National Coal marketing department, who traced them back to Walter. The lower set turned up at a coal merchant's and were handed back.

'Unbelievable,' was Walter's comment. 'After I'd washed them they were as good as new.'

Weekend

ENTERPRISE

WITHIN an easy stone's throw of the Law Society there was an establishment which announced its business in bold letters, on a plate-glass window: 'Facsimile typing and duplicating service. Typists to the legal profession.'

Recently there seems to have been a change of policy. The window is now full of nyloned legs, seductive nightdresses and dainty articles of feminine underwear, but the business description is unchanged.

Solicitors' Journal

Boys' stretchable T-shirts are Fashion's new snap-on clips that transform your daytime glasses into evening gaiety.

Advert in *San Diego Tribune*

The police announce that dogs without dollars found wandering after 10 p.m. are liable to be destroyed.

Hong Kong paper

Miss Gorman, in a quiet part as a nice woman, makes it obvious that she is a very good actress indeed.

Canadian paper

I had to catch the first train in the morning that would get me to the frontier, and arranged with the hotel that I should be soused at 5 o'clock.

South African magazine

James Ward, R.A., gained the prize, but being too large to hang his painting was rolled up and placed in Chelsea Hospital.

Trade publication

FOR SALE. One big elephant wagon, holds two elephants, or would suit showman.

Advert in *World's Fair*

'We are going at it hammer and tongs to make all the buns we can,' said the baker.

Sunderland Echo

A medical journal in 1956 reported the case of a man who was involved in a minor explosion when he hiccupped while lighting a cigarette. The only damage done was a slight singeing of his moustache.

His doctor traced the cause to the operation he had had a few weeks before. This had left him with an excess of a powerful gas in his stomach which ignited on being hiccupped into the flame of a match.

Reveille

A haggis, which arrived at Sao Paulo, Brazil, this week, so puzzled customs officials that they called in their analytical chemist.

His verdict: The contents could be classified under 'Unscheduled horticulture fertilizers.' The haggis was admitted duty-free.

Daily Mirror

WE INFORM ALL HAULIERS AND CITIZENS WHO HAVE CATTLE THAT THEIR PRESENCE IN A DRUNKEN CONDITION IN STATIONS AND TRAINS IS FORBIDDEN

Notice on North Caucasus Railway

A firm of paper manufacturers offered me, 'as a member of the catering and hotels profession', twelve dozen toilet rolls in attractive pastel shades at reduced prices for my guests.

I run a boarding kennels for dogs and cats.

Mr E. Thorn, Rugby.

Daily Mirror

This lovely dress in satin and lace has a matching waist-length jacket. The lace skirt comes off for less formal occasions.

Herts paper

. . . and therefore, as the fathers have eaten sour grapes, the children's teeth are set on hedges.

West African paper

The Ministry of Agriculture said: 'Everything is two to three weeks ahead in the farming world. Best lot of lambs we've seen in years and they will soon be pulling rhubarb.'

Daily Mail

In Sheffield a Ministry of Labour official said: 'We are sitting on a razor's edge and it will be some time before we can assess the full effect of any stoppage.'

News of the World

The first swallow has arrived at Devizes. It was spotted by Police Constable John Cooke of Seend, whose hobby is bird-watching, sitting wet and bedraggled on telephone wires at the Prison Bridge, Devizes, on Sunday.

Western Gazette

Q. Is there a right and wrong way to make starch for general ironing purposes?

A. This is the right way. Add two tablespoonfuls of water to six tablespoonfuls of cold water and mix into a thin paste. Stir in boiling water until the starch clarifies.

Belfast Telegraph

To The Under Secretary
Chancellor Exchequer Office
Victoria Embankment,
London

Dear Sir,
I have discovered what is the elixir of life.
It is plug tobacco and nitric acid.
The tobacco is dissolved by the nitric acid
Nitric acid pure is obtained from nitre.
It alone can dissolve plug tobacco.
The solution is the elixir of life.
The discovery is a valuable one and should be profitable.

I am
yours faithfully,
James O'Duffy

Mr V. Gramby will lie down on pieces of broken glass with his naked back. On his breast will be placed a stone weighing 1,800 lbs., and two blacksmiths will break the stone to pieces. Mr V. Gramby will lie down on twelve very sharp swords, and on his breast four persons will stand. Mr V. Gramby will jump down from a height of 7 ft. on pieces of broken glass.

Mr V. Gramby will stop the beating of his heart for a time, and at the same time the pulse of one of his hands will not act, while the pulse of the other will beat at the rate of 220 per minute. Mr V. Gramby will stick long steel pins into several parts of his body, for instance his lungs, throat, and tongue.

Advert in Zanzibar paper

Accountant, solicitor, perfect; £25

Advert in weekly paper

Sir, – In reply to Mr Yarham's letter in Saturday's *Eastern Daily Press*, I would like to point out that the cuckoo heard by my niece on Saturday week and the one I heard and saw on Monday was not riding a cycle when I saw it fly out of a tree.

Eastern Daily Press

BUSINESS LADY requires Comfortable Bed Sitting room with boar.

Advert in Lancs paper

WHY BREAK YOUR CHINA WASHING UP?
Do it automatically in a dishwasher!
From John R. Fordham, Epping. 'Phone 33.
Established 1923.

Advert in *Surrey Mirror*

A two-year-old Sheffield boy, hospital today after swallowing Graham Cotton was taken to aspirin tablets at his home.

Sheffield paper

CAT carrying basket urgently required.

Heaton Chapel Guardian

Accumulated debs are the result of bad planning.

Irish News

Visiting a camp where he had made friends with an Eskimo a few months before, and not finding him, Mr Wilkins inquired after his health. He was told that the man was dead, and the manner of his death was this. One day the deceased came across a member of the tribe fashioning a knife out of the copper which is found in this region. He chaffed him, it appears, on his want of skill. 'You don't know the first thing about making a knife,' he said in effect. The artificer said nothing until he had finished his work, when, remarking, 'I think it is a pretty good knife,' he plunged it into the breast of his critic. The Eskimos have a keen sense of humour, and this incident was much appreciated.

North London paper

At Holsworthy Pigeon Show on Thursday, Mr R. F. Kingston of Bath, won second with a red beard, fourth with a blue bald head, and v.h.c. with a mealy bald head; he was also third in the any other variety class with a yellow beard.

Somerset paper

Under the heading of Worthynbury in Flintshire, it is recorded that 'the Recompence to a Virgin, who had been seduced, is very singular: on Complaint that she was deserted by her Lover, it was ordered by the Court, that she was to lay hold of the Tail of a Bull of three years old, introduced through a Wicker-Door, and shaven and well greased. Two men were to goad the beast: if she could, by Dint of Strength, retain the Bull, she was to have it by Way of Satisfaction; if not, she got nothing but the Grease that remained in her Hands.' Sir Percy Winfield's observation on this passage is that 'Blount's treatment of this law as a compensation for outraged virginity is misleading. It was much more likely a punishment for unchastity.' Certainly the inducement to lay complaint was small enough for any save the most muscular of ex-virgins. But then it used to be a man's world.

from *Miscellany-at-Law* by R. E, Megarry Q.C.

FARR, Edward – Select Poultry, chiefly devotional, of the reign of Queen Elizabeth.

Book catalogue

As the Mayor and his followers entered the church, the choir and congregation sang the morning in his gold chain, cocked hat and National Anthem.

Surrey Times

The Mayor-Elect presided, and to him fell the duty of proposing the death of the Mayor, which he did in felicitous terms.

Local paper

Fog and smog rolled over Los Angeles today, closing two airports and slowing snails to a traffic pace.

Los Angeles paper

Mr Fern demonstrates spinning and weaving undyed fleece into coffee and cream.

Advert in *The Scotsman*

SATURDAY NIGHT DANCE
VERY EXCLUSIVE
☛ Everybody welcome ☚

Notice outside dance hall

It is the Hyacinth which in the past has laid the lion's share of golden eggs for the Dutch nurserymen.

Dutch bulb catalogue

I'll never forget my first kiss. I was 65 at the time and was having a snooze on the Fish Hoek beach when I got kissed. I looked up and saw a large dog running away.

Letter in *Cape Times Weekend Magazine*

Dear Madam,

Please ixcuse Tommy today. He won't come to skule because he is acting as timekeeper for his father, and it is your fault. You gave him an ixample if a fild is 6 miles round, how long will it take a man walking 3½ miles an hour to walk 2½ times round it. Tommy ain't a man so we had to send his father. They went early this morning and father will walk round and Tommy will time him, but please don't give my boy such ixamples again, because my husband must go to work every day to support his family.

Yrs truly, Mrs V. S—

From *Blunders & Howlers* by W. Jerrold

MULES MUST WEAR NAPPIES – BY ORDER

A mayor is having trouble with his 'keep our streets tidy' campaign. His police chief has resigned and local mule owners are in revolt. . . .

All because Mayor Heltor Rocha ordered that all mules passing through the town of Angra Dos Reis, Brazil, must wear NAPPIES. Police Chief Euripides Da Silva said the rule is impossible to enforce – and handed in his badge.

Senhor Adriano Siqueira, who owns 110 mules, said yesterday: 'I can't afford to buy nappies for all my animals. Think of the size! And at least three a day will be necessary.'

Daily Mirror

IF IT'S SWEETS TRY US
The Best is none too good

Confectioner's advert

Will some generously disposed person give to this old established Training Ship for boys of good character only, an Upright Piano?

Advert in evening paper

BABY SHOW. – Best Baby under Six Months; Best Baby under Twelve Months; Best Baby under Two Years; Best Baby under Three Years. Rules for Exhibitors:– All Exhibits become the property of the Committee as soon as staged, and will be sold for the benefit of the Hospital at the termination of the exhibition.

Exhibition programme

While staying near Crewkerne, in Somerset, a hayrick caught fire.

Sunday paper

That night he sat, feet up on the mantelpiece, pipe in mouth, absorbed in the latest issue of a periodical devoted to radio. Beside him the collie lay on the hearth-rug, with his long nose resting on his master's foot.

From a novel

The Sagona's doctors and nurses were scheduled to land last night, but messages indicated that the men probably would be married aboard the ship, receive first-aid treatment, and then be taken to St John's.

New York World-Telegram

U.S. Air Force volunteers, to produce data for space-capsule tolerances, endured rising heat in a controllable chamber. Nude, they reached 400° before feeling pain on the skin. Lightly clothed achieved 450°. Heavy arctic flight gear allowed an easy 500° – the maximum permitted, for fear the clothing would ignite.

Paradoxically, in these dry-air temperatures – sufficient to melt solder at about 370° and to overdo roast beef, which needs only 325° – no great discomfort was felt, due to cooling evaporation of sweat and lung moisture.

True Magazine

CAPTAIN RICHARD JOHNSON, nudist skipper of the nudist ship now lying off Tampa for repairs before it proceeds to the freedom of the Virgin Isles, has at last found a navigator willing to conform with the ship's uniform.

He wires from Cleveland that he will take the post and agree to become nudist 'as soon as the weather abates'.

Daily Express

HOLES PAINTED WHITE
NOT TO BE DRILLED

Notice on aircraft assembly line – *Flight*

More than 100 years ago, when divorce in the modern sense was possible only by Act of Parliament, an unhappily married Town Clerk was promoting a Waterworks Bill for his town; and in clause 64, mingled with something technical about filter beds and stopcocks, appeared the innocent little phrase 'and the Town Clerk's marriage is hereby dissolved'. Nobody could explain how those words got there, and, in fact, nobody ever noticed them while the Bill was going through Parliament, for everyone was fast asleep long before they got to that clause. In due course the Royal Assent was given, and the Town Clerk lived happily ever after.

from *Miscellany-at-Law* by R. E. Megarry, Q.C.

Before the verdict was rendered this morning 'Miss Mexico' told interviewers that if the court freed her, she would become a nut.

Chicago Daily Tribune

'HOODOO' DOGS FLYING
DOCTOR'S AFRICAN PLANES

Rhodesian paper

Wallasey Police issued the following description of a man whose body was recovered from the Mersey, near New Brighton, yesterday morning: Age between 30 and 40, 5 ft 9 in. tall, good build, tattoo on left forearm of woman kneeling on a chair holding a fan, wearing dark striped suit, two print shirts, woollen vest, grey socks and black boots.

Evening Express

Be Thou With Me (Bach) with Organ accpt.
My Heart Ever Faithful (Bach) with Orch. accpt.
Art Thou Troubled with the City of Birmingham Orchestra (Handel).
I'm Going to My Naked Bed (Unaccompanied) – Madrigal.

Concert programme quoted by Fritz Spiegl
in *What the papers didn't mean to say*

. . . and a few moments after the Countess had broken the traditional bottle of champagne on the bows of the noble ship, she slid slowly and gracefully down the slipway, entering the water with scarcely a splash.

Essex paper

A friend of mine kept her rings at night in a saucer of oatmeal on her dressing-table, and one morning when she went to put them on, she found a valuable ring missing. Nobody had been into her room but her husband, who knew nothing about the ring, so here was a deep mystery.

Years later, when repairs were being done to the house, and the bedroom floorboards were taken up, they found the skeleton of a little mouse with the missing ring around its neck. It had gone for the oatmeal, got its head in the ring and couldn't get it off.

Letter in *Cape Times Weekend Magazine*

It has long been a journalistic commonplace, a nutshell maxim in the Fleet Street novitiates that while 'Dog Bites Man' is not news 'Man Bites Dog' is news. . . . If 'Diner Bites Dinner' is not felt at the sub-editor's table to be superlatively newsworthy, 'Dinner Bites Diner' stands in an altogether different class. . . .

There are restaurants in France where you may select your lobster not yet put to the blush by any culinary contact or disguise. In such an establishment a customer complained that the crustacean paraded for his approval was not fresh. Whereupon, according to his evidence, the restaurant proprietor waved it under his nose shouting, 'Not fresh? Smell it!' This invitation he accepted but, so the restaurateur contended, went beyond its terms, peering at it in a manner calculated to cause it annoyance or irritation, so that the sequel was the natural and probable consequence of his own act.

That sequel was that the denizen of the deep, with well-judged precision, reached out a claw and seized the tip of the customer's nose, nor would it let go until it had drawn blood or (as one report suggests) actually removed the extremity of the (to it) intrusive organ, thereby causing the plaintiff pain and suffering and necessitating an operation by a distinguished plastic surgeon (or, as the French so delicately put it 'aesthetic surgeon'). The court found against the restaurateur and ordered him to pay the Franc equivalent of £100 damages and a £3 fine.

from *Straws in My Wig* by Richard Roe

No. 69 One Pair Unique 18th cent. Candlesticks
No. 70 Another Pair, ditto.

Auctioneer's catalogue

He told Mrs X he had a record of the complete works of the Messaiah and she arranged to visit his house the next day to hear it.

'I was playing the Messaiah for about 10 minutes when she said this was not the right occasion for such music,' he went on. 'She started to make overtures to me.'

News of the World

WAITRESSES for breakfast: 7 a.m. to 11 a.m. St. James Court Hotel, Buckingham Gate, SW1. Apply Head Waiter.

Advert in *South London Press*

Pedigree Friesian Ewes, in calf to Pedigree Friesian Bull.

Advert in New Zealand paper

EARS PIERCED WHILST YOU WAIT

Notice in Somerset jeweller's shop

Despite evaporation, the Chowilla dam would be of immense benefit to SA and other States, SA's representative on the River Murray Commission (Mr J. R. Dridan) said yesterday.

He was commenting on a letter to *The Advertiser* from Mr H. O. Hannaford of Kingswood, who said that most of the damned water would be spread over shallow depths and lost.

The Advertiser

Incredible as it may appear, a person will attend at the Monument, and will, for the sum of £2,500, undertake to jump clear of the said Monument; and in coming down will drink some beer and eat a cake, act some trades, shorten and make sail, and bring ship safe to anchor. As soon as the sum stated is collected the performance will take place; and if not performed, the money will be returned to the subscribers.

The Times, Aug 22, 1827

In the following narrative of accidents which have fallen to the lot of one man, now perfectly sound and hearty, and in his 45th year, it is almost necessary for me to premise that the subject (or hero, if you please) of this letter, is very much engaged in horse-breaking, from which dangerous employment most of these misfortunes have arisen. 1. Right shoulder broken to pieces; 2. Scull fractured and trepanned; 3. Left arm broken in two places; 4. Three ribs on the left side broken – a cut in the forehead – lancet-case, flue-case, and knife forced into the thigh. 5. Three ribs broken on the right side – and the right shoulder, elbow, and wrist dislocated; 6. Back dislocated; 7. Scull fractured and trepanned; 8. Cap of the right knee knocked off; 9. Left ancle out; 10. Cut for a fistula; 11. Right ancle out, and hip knocked down; 12. Seven ribs broken on the right and left sides; 13. Cap of the right knee kicked off; 14. Kicked in the face, and the left eye out of socket; 15. Back dislocated; 16. Two ribs and breast-bone broken; 17. Got down by a horse and kicked till he had five holes in his left leg, the sinew just below the right knee cut through, and two holes that leg, and also two shocking cuts above the knee.

He has been taken apparently dead seven times out of different rivers. Besides the above, he has had many other kicks, bruises, and other accidents.

As several of your friends, many of whom live in this neighbourhood, may wish to satisfy themselves of the veracity of the foregoing ennumeration, I shall give them that opportunity, by informing them that Mr George Talkington of Uttoxeter is the person alluded to.

Kirby's Wonderful & Eccentric Museum

Dublin is asking what it all means. Meanwhile, with the political position very much in the dark, the public welcomes the one great fact, which needs no translation into plainer terms – the suspension of histolities.

Glasgow paper

We are pleased at the way your company undertook the funeral. As nicely and calmly as possible. To the extent that even the heavy showers of rain did not start until after we got home.

Letter to undertaker

The banquet was served at a horse-shaped table.

Surrey paper

A lady was sued in the Canterbury County Court over a £7 10s. dress bill. The hearing was adjourned for an inquiry into her means, since she had arrived in a friend's Rolls-Royce and the court, instead of treating this as an inevitable setting for her blonde good looks, tended to regard it suspiciously as a *marque extérieure de la richesse*. The case was reported in the Press, complete with photograph, and before the next hearing an anonymous Frenchman had paid the sum into court. 'Women of such beauty in my country,' he wrote, 'are never guilty. I am sending the money, but if it has been paid, please get her some perfume.'

It had not been paid and His Honour Judge Neal was spared an interesting shopping expedition. Unsentimentally he made an order for the payment of two guineas costs within a month.

Solicitors' Journal

Humour

Compiled by Roger Brook with drawings by Timothy Birdsall

REALLY NURSE! and WAKE UP, NURSE! 17½p

Denys Parsons

FUNNY AMUSING AND FUNNY AMAZING 17½p

Revilo Snivib

WHAT'S UP DOC ? (illus) 20p

Louis Untermeyer

THE PAN BOOK OF LIMERICKS 25p

Playboy Cartoon Books

Brian Savage

SO THIS IS LOVE! 25p

WE CAN'T GO ON MEETING LIKE THIS 25p

Howard Shoemaker

GOODBYE CRUEL WORLD 25p

DOCTOR! DOCTOR! 25p

WHY DO I GET AN IRRESISTIBLE URGE TO LAUGH EVERY TIME I MAKE LOVE? 25p

NOT UNTIL YOU TAKE OFF THAT SILLY HAT 25p

Play your cards right!

BRIDGE FOR BEGINNERS

Victor Mollo and Nico Gardener 25p

This excellent book is for the complete beginner. It explains every phase of bridge step by step – the rules, scoring, the conventions and techniques of bidding and card play. And there are exercises after each lesson to help the reader develop his newly acquired skill.

THE COMPLETE PATIENCE BOOK

Basil Dalton 30p

Here are three best-selling Patience books for the price of one! Incorporating the author's GAMES OF PATIENCE, DOUBLE PACK PATIENCE and PATIENCE PROBLEMS AND PUZZLES, it includes over one hundred different games of Patience. Some are easy, some are difficult – all provide a unique form of mental exercise and entertainment.

Puzzle Books

MATHEMATICAL GAMES

C. Lukács and E. Tarján 25p

Here is a book that proves mathematics *can* be fun!

'This is a book for the whole family, with games which can provide endless hours of amusement for any number of players' – HULL DAILY MAIL

'Nothing seems to have been left out... those who like to spend their surplus intellectual energy on mathematical games and problems will not find a page wasted' – THE ACCOUNTANT

MAZES

Vladimir Kozlakin 40p

How bright are you? Flex your mental muscles with the most challenging game of the year. Ideal for parties, commuters, nightowls lighthouse keepers and solitary puzzlers.

These and other PAN Books are obtainable from all booksellers and newsagents. If you have any difficulty please send purchase price plus 7p postage to PO Box 11, Falmouth, Cornwall.

While every effort is made to keep prices low, it is sometimes necessary to increase prices at short notice. PAN Books reserve the right to show new retail prices on covers which may differ from those advertised in the text or elsewhere.